W9-CAT-670

ELEPHANT TALK

THE SURPRISING SCIENCE OF ELEPHANT COMMUNICATION

ANN DOWNER

 TWENTY-FIRST CENTURY BOOKS • MINNEAPOLIS

This book is dedicated to Jeheskel "Hezy" Shoshani, 1943–2008, and to the elephants.

Twenty-First Century Books
A division of Lerner Publishing Group, Inc.
241 First Avenue North
Minneapolis, MN 55401 U.S.A.

Website address: www.lernerbooks.com

Library of Congress Cataloging-in-Publication Data

Downer, Ann.
    Elephant talk : the surprising science of elephant communication / by Ann Downer.
      p.   cm.
    Includes bibliographical references and index.
    ISBN 978–0–7613–5766–7 (lib. bdg. : alk. paper)
    1. Elephants—Behavior—Juvenile literature. 2. Animal communication—Juvenile literature. 3. Animal societies—Juvenile literature. I. Title.
    QL737.P98D69 2011
    599.67'4159—dc22   2010024880

Manufactured in the United States of America
1 – BP – 12/31/10

| CONTENTS |

INTRODUCTION

A TALE OF
THREE
ELEPHANTS

A SAVANNA ELEPHANT

It is early morning in Amboseli National Park in Kenya, Africa. A baby elephant hurries to keep up with his mother and sisters and aunts as the herd moves out, following the eldest female to a stand of acacia trees. They will spend the morning browsing on acacia bark and grass. As the herd raises a cloud of red dust, white cattle egrets hitch a ride on the rolling shoulders of the massive animals. This herd belongs to one of two species of African elephant, the savanna elephant, named for the grasslands on which they live.

The week-old calf is still figuring out how to put one foot in front of the other. Now and then, he stumbles and trips over his trunk, which dangles limply between his front feet. But already he is part of the herd, a rich and complex society.

This is a herd of African savanna elephants, a species that lives on the grasslands of Africa. This photograph was taken in Amboseli National Park in Kenya.

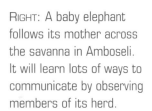

RIGHT: A baby elephant follows its mother across the savanna in Amboseli. It will learn lots of ways to communicate by observing members of its herd.

BELOW: A savanna elephant flaps its large ears.

The calf knows the members of his large family by their scent. He is beginning to learn the meaning of their calls as well as their body language: a curled trunk, a nod, or a flapping ear. His brain is gathering and processing information about his herd, his environment, and other animals. He will have an elephant's unique combination of senses to do this and be aided, much like a human baby, by a long childhood in a close-knit society. As he grows to adulthood, his brain will triple in size. He is built to learn.

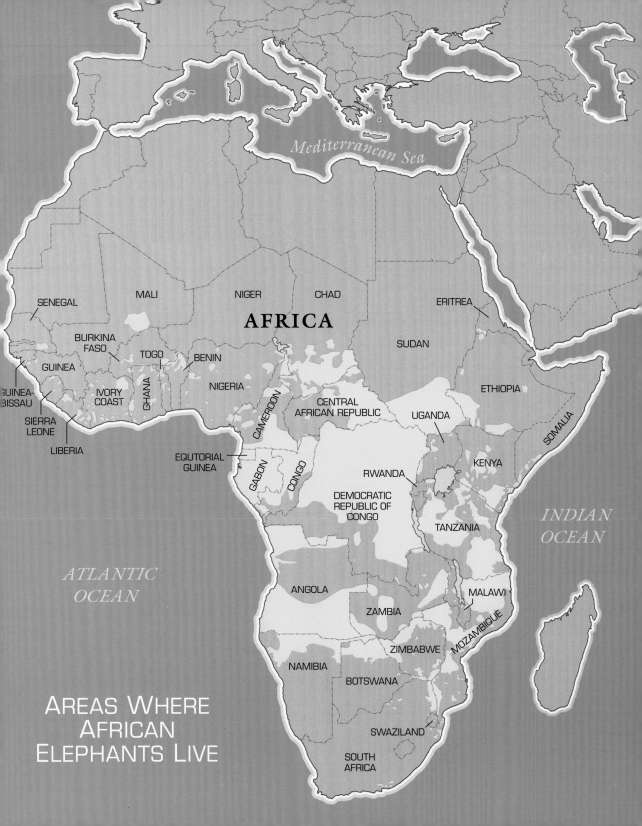

Mediterranean Sea

AFRICA

SENEGAL

MALI

NIGER

CHAD

ERITREA

BURKINA
FASO

TOGO

BENIN

SUDAN

GUINEA

NIGERIA

ETHIOPIA

GUINEA-
BISSAU

IVORY
COAST

GHANA

CAMEROON

CENTRAL
AFRICAN REPUBLIC

UGANDA

SOMALIA

SIERRA
LEONE

LIBERIA

EQUTORIAL
GUINEA

GABON

CONGO

RWANDA

KENYA

DEMOCRATIC
REPUBLIC
OF
CONGO

TANZANIA

INDIAN
OCEAN

ATLANTIC
OCEAN

ANGOLA

MALAWI

ZAMBIA

MOZAMBIQUE

ZIMBABWE

NAMIBIA

BOTSWANA

AREAS WHERE
AFRICAN
ELEPHANTS LIVE

SWAZILAND

SOUTH
AFRICA

A FOREST ELEPHANT

In the Central African Republic, in a remote forest near the border with Cameroon, a small, dark brown elephant with pink tusks is moving through the trees. This is a forest elephant, a member of a shy and still mysterious species. She pauses at the edge of a clearing, her adult eldest daughter and three calves of different ages gathered behind her. One hundred elephants have gathered in this swampy place to drink and dig up the nutrient-rich mud salts. They have been dyed different pastel colors by the various muds they've wallowed in. Using her sense of smell and perhaps recognizing the sounds of elephants she knows, this elephant mother decides it's all right: this is a family reunion. As she leads her offspring into the clearing, they are greeted by their relatives. Sisters and aunts and cousins welcome the newcomers with noisy calls. The calls are picked up by special recording equipment hidden high in the trees around the edges of the

A group of African forest elephants digs up minerals from the mud in this forest clearing in the Central African Republic. Their tusks are tinged pink from the minerals.

clearing. The elephants don't know it, but their very survival may depend on what researchers can learn from these recordings.

AN ASIAN ELEPHANT

Thousands of miles away, in a North American zoo, a thirty-four-year-old female Asian elephant called Daisy is beginning her own day. This morning she is scheduled for a checkup by the zoo's head veterinarian. Her keeper is worried that she might have injured her foot. Daisy's ears swivel this way and that as she monitors the sounds around her. Amid the excited buzz of a group of elementary school students on a field trip, she detects a sound she recognizes. She raises her head and stands very still to listen. It's the motor of the electric jeep that brings the vet to the elephant barn. Shortly thereafter, she hears the vet greeting the elephant barn staff.

Daisy knows the vet's voice, and the elephant gives an anxious rumble. It is picked up by her elder "sisters" Magnolia and Orchid, who offer sympathetic rumbles in return. Magnolia's three-year-old calf Zara thinks it is feeding time and wanders over to the gate to greet the keeper. But Daisy is still anxious.

A forty-year-old Asian elephant named Bamboo receives a foot cleaning from her keeper at the Woodland Park Zoo in Seattle, Washington.

The keeper comes into the elephant barn to move Daisy to the smaller barred enclosure where the medical exam will take place. He is speaking to her in a reassuring voice, and she calms down a little. She can smell apples in his pockets. She snakes the tip of her trunk over his jacket, feeling the outline of the fruit. The vet comes in to the enclosure and greets Daisy, and the keeper gives Daisy the command to lift up her foot. She's been taught to do this so exams will be easier on everyone. The vet determines that Daisy has an infected toenail on one of her front feet. As the vet and the keeper discuss the treatment, Daisy gets her food reward. As she crunches the apple, she flaps her ears in contentment. The worst is over, and it was not so bad.

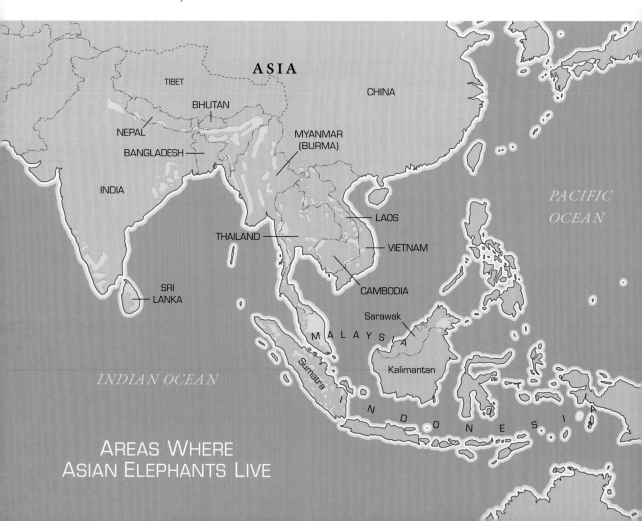

AREAS WHERE
ASIAN ELEPHANTS LIVE

FAST FACTS ABOUT ELEPHANTS

Loxodonta africana (African savanna elephant)
Range: Sub-Saharan Africa, limited to scattered habitats and wildlife reserves
Maximum height: Males, 12 feet (3.6 meters); females, 9 feet (2.7 m)
Maximum weight: 8,000 to 13,000 pounds (3,600 to 6,000 kilograms)
Distinguishing features: Large ears, each up to 4 feet (1 m) across, swayed back, dark gray skin

Loxodonta cyclotis (African forest elephant)
Range: Dense forests of the Congo Basin in Africa
Maximum height: Males, 8.2 feet (2.5 m); females 6.8 feet (2.1 m)
Maximum weight: 6,000 to 13,000 pounds (2,700 to 6,000 kg)
Distinguishing features: Dark brown skin, small pink tusks

Elephas maximus (Asian elephant)
Range: Indian subcontinent and Southeast Asia
Maximum height: Males, 9 feet (2.7 m); females, 8 feet (2.4 m)
Maximum weight: Males, 12,000 pounds (5,400 kg); females, 6,000 pounds (2,700 kg)
Distinguishing features: Small ears, about 16 inches (41 centimeters) wide; rounded back; skin gray brown. Females lack large tusks.
Subspecies: Some scientists recognize elephants of India, Sri Lanka, and Borneo as three subspecies in the genus *Elephas*.

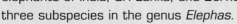

THE ELEPHANT FAMILY TREE
(IT'S COMPLICATED)

The Proboscidea, as the ancient group including elephants is called, arose about 37 million years ago and spread from Africa into Asia. This group developed many fantastic forms—probably none stranger than *Platybelodon*, a 10-foot-high (3 m) animal with tusks like shovels. It looked more like a backhoe than an elephant.

Scientists think that the African elephant split off from the mammoth branch of the tree about 7.6 million years ago. About 1 million years after that, the Asian line split off from mammoths. That means Asian elephants are more closely related to extinct mammoths than they are to African elephants. The closest living relatives to the elephants are believed to be the water-dwelling dugongs and manatees.

Recent DNA studies have shown the genetic differences between the forest and savanna elephants in Africa are great enough that they should actually be considered two separate species. (DNA stands for deoxyribonucleic acid, the unique genetic fingerprint encoded inside each living cell.) Analysis of their genes suggests that the two African elephant species may be less closely related than a lion is to a tiger or a horse is to a zebra.

Despite appearances, most scientists don't consider mammoths (RIGHT) direct ancestors of elephants, although they occupy the same family tree. African elephants and Asian elephants share a common ancestor with the mammoth, but each elephant species evolved separately.

SMART AND SOCIAL

Daisy's environment is very different from the grassy savanna of Amboseli National Park or a forest clearing in the Central African Republic. But like the two wild elephants, Daisy is an intelligent, highly social animal, well adapted to life in a group. She is able to gather and exchange information with her fellow elephants and with her keepers through several means of communication. These include vocalizations (sounds made using the vocal cords and trunk), body language, and her keen sense of smell. She even communicates through walls, using sounds too low for humans to hear and vibrations picked up through her feet.

How and why have these largest of the living land animals developed such complex communication skills? How can we know what they are saying to one another? Are there differences between the way wild and captive elephants "speak"? Can elephants and people communicate? And finally, what answers might the secrets of elephant communication hold for conservationists racing to save these splendid giants from extinction?

LISTENING TO ELEPHANTS

Over the last five thousand years, elephants have joined in religious festivals, guarded temples, and presided over weddings. Wearing elephant armor, they have carried generals into battle. They toiled in teak plantations and helped build the Taj Mahal, a famous royal tomb in India. Elephants carried

This illuminated German manuscript from 1360 shows an elephant in battle. Elephants were used in battle thousands of years ago as well as in modern times as recently as 1885 in the Siamese (Thai) army.

An elephant's head, trunk, and ears are painted in preparation for the Hindu festival of Rath Yatra in Puri, a city in eastern India. Often every inch of an elephant's skin is covered with intricate patterns.

British officers on tiger hunts in the 1800s and early 1900s in India. And they took Hollywood stars on safari in Africa. They captivate audiences at circuses and zoos around the world and star in movies and cartoons, from *Dumbo* to *Operation Dumbo Drop*. They became a symbol of royalty in Thailand and the symbol of the Republican political party in the United States. In 2004 they helped clear rubble after the deadly tsunamis in Asia. It can be argued that no other animal has served so many different roles in human culture as the elephant.

Yet despite elephants' unique role in our shared history, humans are driving these largest of the land animals to extinction—by robbing them of their habitat, leaving them vulnerable to disease, shooting them when they encroach on farms and other settlements, and illegally killing about thirty-five thousand animals a year for their ivory tusks. The poachers (hunters who illegally kill wild animals) shoot the elephant and remove the tusks, leaving the carcass—and often an orphaned calf—behind. Even after an international ban in 1990 prohibiting the sale of ivory, poaching continues in some parts of Africa at the rate of one hundred elephants a day.

To save elephants, scientists say, we need to know much more about them: where and how many there are, how they form relationships with one another, how they use and move about their territories, how often they mate, and how often matings result in a healthy calf. And it seems that one of the keys to understanding elephants is understanding "elephant talk."

Elephant communication turns out to be much more complex and sophisticated than researchers had previously suspected. Scientists are using old-fashioned fieldwork and high-tech science to shed light on elephant society and the role communication plays in the life of the herd.

Elephants have a lot to say, and in the last few decades, scientists have been learning to listen in.

CHAPTER 1

BORN INTO
THE HEART
OF A HERD

Just like many other long-lived, large-brained animals, elephants are born relatively helpless. It takes time for the calf to develop. For the first three months, the infant calf relies on his mother to meet every need. The calf is dependent on his mother for milk, protection, and reassurance. The baby is clumsy and still learning to move with the herd. He spends a lot of time safe within the sturdy pillars of his mother's legs, comforted by her warmth, her sounds, and her smell.

At the beginning of his fourth month, the calf enters a kind of elephant toddlerhood. He becomes more aware of his environment and what it means to be an elephant. He may play with straw and try to gather grass or leaves, or he may imitate his mother when she takes a dust bath or shower. He is beginning to sample the leaves and brush that elephants eat and to play at foraging (scouting) for them. The calf will continue to nurse until he is at least six months old. During that time, an aunt or an older sister acting as a foster

At Amboseli National Park in Kenya, the leader of this elephant herd lifts her trunk to smell for danger. The young elephant to the right imitates her.

mother may occasionally take over nursing duties. She does this for comfort, not nourishment, as these foster mothers don't produce milk.

As he grows, the calf will depend more and more on a wider network of older brothers and sisters, aunts and, most important, the matriarch of the herd. The matriarch is the top-ranking female, usually the oldest and most experienced elephant. She makes most decisions about life in the herd. Below her in rank are the next oldest females.

At nine months, the calf begins to venture from his mother's side, spending more time interacting with other calves and juveniles. He is learning where he fits in among the other calves. Learning to be around other elephants his own age is a lot like going off to elephant school and learning who's who on the playground. The calf chases and wrestles with his sisters and plays splashing

Young elephants in Addo Elephant National Park in South Africa wrestle. Young elephants play and observe older elephants as they learn the ways of the herd.

games at the watering hole. He is beginning to master body language. He may run and fan his ears to startle cattle, like a human child chasing pigeons.

Finally, the calf enters his "teen" years around the age of eight or nine, when he shows greater independence. He has grown much bigger than his sisters and female cousins the same age. His sisters will remain with the herd when they reach sexual maturity some time between the ages of nine and fifteen. When the young male begins to show signs of sexual maturity, the calf's mother or the matriarch will drive him away. He will most likely join a small group of fellow bachelors.

BEYOND HERDS

Wild elephants live in family groups called herds. But each elephant herd is part of a widening circle of social networks. Some of these are blood ties, relationships with family members that are stable and unchanging. Others are bonds created by conditions in the environment—a shift in the leadership of another family group, perhaps, or a change in the availability of food.

The most basic unit of savanna elephant society is the family, a group of related females and their immature calves. Families may be as small as a mother and her calf or as large as sixteen elephants—a mature female, or cow, her adult sisters and daughters, and their calves. The matriarch makes most of the decisions for the family group. She's the one to assess threats, choose allies (friends), and decide where to eat and when to move.

Elephant families sometimes join larger groups of up to fifty elephants, called a bond group. The bond group may be a neighboring herd of other elephants, perhaps more distantly related, that join with the central family group for a day or two. Research has shown that mothers and daughters tend to stick together, but cousins split apart. Even though bond group members aren't as closely related as members of the smaller family groups, they still all cooperate. They will join forces against predators and help raise one another's calves. Many factors can cause these bond groups to split. These include the availability of food and water during a drought, the death of a matriarch, and even personality clashes among bond group members.

THE GRANDMOTHER ADVANTAGE

Evolutionary biologists (scientists who study how living organisms have evolved) have long wondered why the female of the species lives past her reproductive years—growing old after she can no longer produce young. After all, salmon and many other fish die soon after laying their eggs. Some mayflies spend a single day in their adult forms. Why would it make sense for some animals to live into old age, especially a large animal like an elephant, which lives in an environment where food can be scarce?

In the case of humans, the answer may be the evolutionary advantage of grandmothers. In the deep past, a woman whose prime reproductive years were behind her didn't have to devote her efforts to finding a mate. She could invest that time and energy helping her daughters raise their offspring. She also contributed to the tribe in other ways, with her knowledge of local fauna (animals), other tribes, weather patterns, and the best place to forage (scout) for edible plants. She was a storehouse of cultural memory.

Evidence suggests a similar advantage may hold true for elephant grandmothers. Female elephants can live for decades after the birth of their last calf, in a phase not unlike the female human experience of menopause. Studying elephants in Amboseli National Park in Kenya, researcher Karen McComb found that older females built up "social memories." They were better able to tell friend from foe, and herds with these wise grandmothers raised more calves. It seems elephant herds may have more success reproducing when they can rely on the memory and wisdom of their matriarch and the other grandmothers.

A grandmother and her grandson in Southeast Asia

The highest level of elephant society is the clan. These are the families that are willing to share the same foraging area when food is scarce. Clan groups are usually stable and can last with few changes as long as thirty years. In times of plenty, neighboring clans can join together into groups of hundreds of elephants.

BULL ELEPHANT SOCIETY

Another elephant group is the band of males that forms when inexperienced bull elephants leave their birth herd and join with other males to form bachelor societies. Because earlier elephant research had focused on the matriarch and her herd, it had long been thought that bull elephants wandered alone or in small groups, looking for mates. Research in Namibia on the society of these all-male groups is changing this picture. Bull elephant societies may have their own hierarchies and struggles for power. But they have a gentler side too. Males form strong bonds, and older bulls serve as mentors to younger bulls.

An adult male (FRONT) and a younger male African forest elephant find food in the Central African Republic. Male, or bull, elephants form groups just as females and calves do.

STUDYING SCAT

One of the ways scientists learn about elephant societies is by studying elephant dung. Call it poop, scat, or feces, there is certainly plenty of it scattered around the study site! An African elephant can produce between 300 and 540 pounds (about 135 to 245 kg) of it a day. Scientists can even use the size of an elephant dropping to calculate the size of the elephant that left it.

Dung analysis can reveal details about an elephant's diet and whether the elephant is infected with parasites. Researchers can use it to measure the levels of certain hormones—chemicals produced in the body—that coordinate the elephants' drive to mate. Scat is also a convenient way to sample an animal's DNA, the unique genetic fingerprint encoded inside each living cell.

In 1997 graduate student Beth Archie of Duke University in North Carolina was studying the African savanna elephant herds at Amboseli National Park in Kenya. She wanted to know if dung could reveal more about elephant relationships than researchers could gather through observation alone. So she put down her binoculars, put on a pair of rubber gloves, and collected hundreds and hundreds of samples of elephant scat in plastic vials between 1997 and 2005.

Stable bull elephant societies may be important to reducing incidents of human-elephant and interspecies conflict. Some evidence suggests that aggression in young bull elephants is controlled by the presence of older males. In the early 1990s, young male savanna elephants were orphaned when some of their herd was culled, or killed to reduce the elephant population, in the Kruger Park game reserve in South Africa. Because elephants eat so much vegetation, when herds in nature reserves become too large, they can strip the land of plants. With no plants to eat, the elephants and other animals would starve. When this happens, park

Archie wanted to see if the dung could reveal how the elephants were related. Her findings confirmed that bonds formed by a female elephant and her daughters and sisters can last for generations. The research also suggested that the close family bonds helped ensure that younger females successfully raised their own calves. Poaching breaks those long-term family ties.

More recently, researchers have been checking elephant scat for levels of stress hormones. They want to determine how elephants are affected by ever-closer human settlements and by tourism. Conservationists have even created a database of elephant dung samples that can be used to identify the source of poached ivory. DNA from confiscated tusks can be matched to DNA from elephant dung in the database.

Jason Munshi-South takes a sample of elephant dung from forest elephants in Gabon.

officials may perform a cull (the act of controlling the size of a herd by killing or removing some animals). However, not all experts agree with this practice.

The orphans were relocated to a neighboring game reserve in Pilanesberg. Growing up without elephant father figures, the young elephants began to display highly unusual, aggressive behaviors. They attacked and killed two people and killed more than forty white rhinos.

After wildlife managers transferred six older bull elephants from Kruger Park, the aggressive behavior by the young delinquent elephants at Pilanesberg stopped. Introduction of older males into the group appeared to reduce the younger elephants' levels of aggression.

FUSING AND SPLITTING

Scientists who study animal behavior call this pattern of herds that form, split, and reform fusion-fission societies. Studies of herd members' DNA have shown that two herds are more likely to fuse, or join, when their matriarchs are related. Scientists aren't sure why African savanna elephants have this flexible social arrangement, but it may have to do with changing conditions in their environment. During the rainy season, it may make sense to gather in a bigger group to help protect against predators such as lions. But once the dry season arrives and food becomes scarce, the herd may split up and spread out to make better use of scattered patches of food. Researchers think that the need to stay in touch over large distances and reunite the family after separation has been important in shaping the many forms of elephant communication.

Two groups of elephants exchange greetings while reuniting at a watering hole in Chobe National Park of Botswana.

John Ford listens to orca whale sounds at the Vancouver Aquarium in British Columbia, Canada. Orcas and other large-brained mammals such as elephants are social animals. Studying all kinds of social animals helps further understanding of their behaviors.

WHAT MAKES AN ANIMAL SOCIAL?

Over the last twenty-five years, scientists who study animal behavior began to realize that animal societies as different as whales and lions, apes and elephants, and parrots and bats had some traits in common. Among the mammals and birds, social animals tend to have longer life spans and larger than average brains compared to similar species that are not highly social. Scientists began to suspect that large brains somehow helped social animals manage the complexities of social life. They studied sociality in apes and other primates and such marine mammals as killer whales and dolphins. Then they began to look at sociality in other large-brained, long-lived species. Elephants stood out.

BIG BRAINS

Elephants were a good candidate for studies of sociality. African savanna elephants have the largest brains of all land animals, and the elephant life span can be as long as sixty-five years. Elephants are known to share groups of behaviors that are common in other animal societies. These include:

OVERLAPPING GENERATIONS LIVING TOGETHER

Elephant herds are made up of two or three generations of related individuals.

GROUP DEFENSE

The group works together to defend resources against rival groups and to repel attacks by predators.

COOPERATIVE REARING OF YOUNG

Elephants band together to defend calves against lions and other predators. They will join to pull infants out of ditches or rescue them from other trouble. Females will even nurse calves that aren't their own.

Two female elephants watch over a newborn calf in Kenya. The mother and other females in the herd share child-rearing duties.

FORMING COALITIONS

Many social animals, such as hyenas, apes, and dolphins, form alliances with other members of the group to climb the social ladder. Female elephants learn to maneuver among a complex set of relationships, competing and cooperating with other females. Once males leave their birth herd, they form groups with other males and spend a lot of time jockeying for dominance (leadership in the herd).

Elephants also exhibit some behaviors shared by very few other animals. These behaviors are thought to be hallmarks of the high intelligence some scientists believe is linked to sociality:

TOOL USE

In the early 1990s, researchers reported possible tool use in both captive and wild savanna and Asian elephants. Elephants have been observed using clumps of grass like Q-tips to clean out their ear canals and fashioning pieces of fence posts to dislodge leeches, among dozens of other behaviors.

An elephant calf uses a clump of grass to scratch its forehead.

SELF-MEDICATION WITH MEDICINAL PLANTS

In the 1970s, ecologist Holly Dublin of the World Wildlife Fund witnessed an elephant that went 17 miles (27 kilometers) out of her way to browse on a certain species of tree the day before she gave birth. This raised the intriguing possibility that something in the tree's bark and leaves served to induce labor. Elephants also go to great lengths to dig up and eat mineral-rich clay that may help counteract the effects of toxic compounds in the plants they eat—antacid for elephants!

MOURNING

Many wildlife managers and elephant researchers have remarked on the high level of interest elephants display toward elephant bones, touching them with their feet and trunks. They do not do this with the bones of other species. Some researchers see this as a sign of mourning.

SIMBA'S BRAIN

Evidence that has emerged over the last fifteen years suggests that it's not just the size of the brain that makes some animals—from humans to apes, whales to elephants—social. It appears that the brains of highly social vertebrates (animals having a backbone) may be different in a more basic way—at the level of their cells.

In 1995 Esther Nimchinsky and Patrick Hof, two scientists at Mount Sinai School of Medicine in New York, observed some unusually shaped nerve cells in the human brain they were studying. They realized they were looking at a spindle neuron, a type of brain cell first described in 1926.

These neurons were strikingly different from ordinary human brain cells. Where most neurons were short, with many branches to transmit nerve signals, the spindle neurons were long and only had branches on each end.

Nimchinsky and Hof wondered if spindle cells might have evolved to help early humans cope with the demands of their bigger brains. Bigger brains meant that the messages sent by nerves had greater distances to cross. What if spindle cells worked like a megaphone, allowing the nervous system to deliver its messages across these bigger brains more quickly and efficiently?

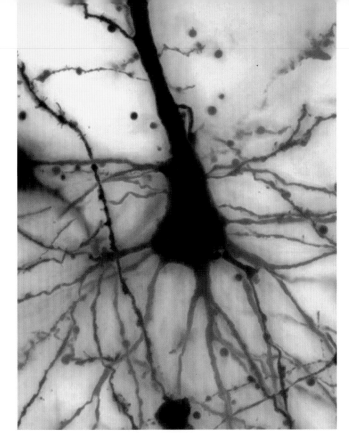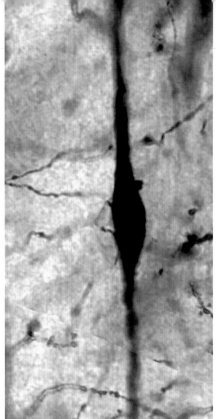

These images show a typical neuron (LEFT) and a spindle neuron (RIGHT). Spindle neurons are long and have branches only at the ends. Research has shown that spindle neurons can be found in the brains of several species of highly social animals as well as in the brains of people.

To find out if the neurons were limited to human brains, the Mount Sinai team asked for help from colleagues working on the brains of nonhuman primates. Researchers around the world sent in samples from the brains of twenty-eight species of monkeys and apes. Nimchinsky and Hof found spindle neurons in all the great ape brains but in none of the monkey brains. Interestingly, the neurons were abundant in the brains of humans and chimpanzees and frequent in gorillas—all highly social species. But they were rarer in the brains of the much more solitary orangutan. Further research turned up spindle neurons in the brains of whales, dolphins, and both African savanna and Asian elephants.

YOU CAN'T TAKE AN
ELEPHANT'S BRAIN ON A PLANE

Back in 2006, word reached researchers in John Allman's lab at the California Institute of Technology (Caltech) that the Cleveland Zoo in Ohio had a couple of elephant brains to donate for research. If the lab wanted the brains, they would have to come to Cleveland to prepare them for shipment. Researcher Atiya Hakeem was offered the assignment, and she and her husband set out for Cleveland.

They arrived to confront two elephant brains in 5-gallon (19-liter) buckets of formalin—a chemical preservative with powerful fumes that must be used with plenty of ventilation. The brains had been divided into hemispheres (halves), each neatly sliced "like a loaf of bread," Hakeem recalls. "We had to reassemble the slices like a jigsaw to make sure we had the whole thing."

The slices of elephant brain were repacked individually in plastic sandwich bags in a solution of ordinary table salt and water—a good enough preservative to get them to Caltech. Five bags of brain slices were sealed into another, larger zip-top bag. The large bags went into two metal flour canisters and the canisters into a Tupperware tub. Even though the two scientists were using salt to pack the brains, the formalin fumes in the lab still got to them. "Every once in a while we went out into the corridor and had a coughing fit from the formalin," Hakeem noted. The Tupperware tub went into a special Styrofoam mailer, and by day's end, they delivered their box to the FedEx counter. Hakeem said, "We marked the form 'biological specimens'—we weren't about to write 'elephant brains'!"

John Allman (LEFT) and Atiya Hakeem (RIGHT) examine thin slices of elephant brain tissue.

John Allman and Atiya Hakeem, scientists at the California Institute of Technology, studied the brain of a zoo elephant named Simba. Examining paper-thin slices of the elephant's brain, they found spindle neurons much larger than those found in humans and great apes. The spindle neurons in Simba's brain were about as large as the spindle neurons found in the brains of whales. The presence of spindle neurons in a number of highly social species suggested they might play a social role. But more evidence was needed.

A vital clue to the role the neurons might play in the social lives of animals with large brains has come from an unexpected source: Alzheimer's research. Alzheimer's disease seems to target the social centers of the brain, and patients often lose the ability to interact with others in meaningful ways. When researchers looked at the brains of people who had died from Alzheimer's disease, they found that almost all their spindle neurons in a region of the brain thought to process emotions had been destroyed. By wiping out the spindle neurons, Alzheimer's disease seemed to be erasing the social center of the brain.

The growing body of research into elephant intelligence and sociality is fostering a new appreciation of the rich and complex lives elephants lead and why they have evolved so many different channels of communication. Understanding how elephant societies function is also proving crucial to keeping them healthy and happy in captivity. It is shaping efforts to save remaining elephant populations in the wild.

CHAPTER 2

TRUMPETS,
RUMBLES,
AND LONG-
DISTANCE CALLS

The trumpet—the loud, bugling call an elephant makes by blowing air forcibly through its trunk—is a sound familiar to anyone who has seen an elephant in the movies or at a zoo or who has been lucky enough to observe one in the wild. But the trumpet is only one of more than seventy vocalizations (sounds made with voice) an elephant uses to express itself and get its point across to family members, unrelated elephants, and other animals. Some of the calls elephants make fall within the range of human hearing. Other calls are too low for humans to hear.

With a vocal range of about ten octaves (three more than a piano!), elephants can produce an astonishing variety of sounds. In groundbreaking work with African savanna elephants at Kenya's Amboseli National Park, Joyce Poole and her colleagues have identified ten basic call types. Seven are produced in the larynx or the throat: the bark, the cry, the grunt, the husky cry, the rev, the roar, and the rumble. Three additional calls are produced in the trunk: the trumpet, the nasal-trumpet, and the snort. (You can hear all these calls by visiting Poole's website ElephantVoices.) By combining these basic calls, savanna elephants are able to produce at least seventy distinct calls.

This African savanna elephant lets loose a mighty trumpet.

THE ELEPHANT'S SPECIAL VOCAL EQUIPMENT

Elephants and humans share the same basic vocal apparatus. The lungs expel air, which travels up the windpipe, or trachea, to the larynx. There it causes the vocal cords, or folds, to vibrate. The throat and open spaces in the skull called sinuses act as echo chambers to amplify the sounds even further. (Try speaking with your nose pinched to hear the difference that air flowing freely through your sinuses makes to the sound of your voice.)

An elephant has some additional equipment that helps it produce loud sounds. Scientists think the elephant's powerful trumpeting is helped by three aspects of elephant anatomy. First, everything about the elephant is bigger, from the lungs that send a blast of air to the vocal cords to the massive skull with its extensive echo chamber of sinus cavities. Second, the vocal cords are unusually loose and flexible, which allows them to move more freely. Finally, an elephant's 7-foot long (2 m) trunk acts like a horn or a trumpet when air is blasted through it. A special pouch behind the elephant's tongue, called the pharyngeal pouch, helps elephants produce low sounds.

Does an elephant really trumpet like a trumpet? Research from a zoo in France says yes, but it's more like a trombone. The long trunk, loose vocal cords, and powerful lungs all add up to a blast that mimics a brass instrument. This diagram shows the structures the elephant uses to vocalize and process scents in its environment.

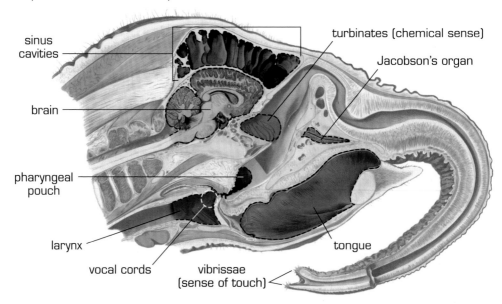

sinus cavities

turbinates (chemical sense)

Jacobson's organ

brain

pharyngeal pouch

larynx

vocal cords

vibrissae (sense of touch)

tongue

A MOST AMAZING APPENDAGE

What good is an elephant's trunk? Well, it's excellent for greeting friends with a wave or by trumpeting, "How've you been?" The trumpeting can tell an unwelcome stranger or hyena to get lost. And it's unmatched at smelling. It is about five hundred times more sensitive to airborne odors than the nose of a bloodhound. An elephant can also use its trunk to get a cool drink, to take a shower or a dust bath, or to get mud out of its eye after a roll in the local wallow. Baby elephants even suck the ends of their trunks the way some babies suck their thumbs!

The equivalent of our nose and upper lip, the elephant's trunk is both exquisitely sensitive and amazingly strong. The fingerlike extension on the end of the trunk allows the elephant to pluck a single blade of grass or retrieve objects as small as a coin from the ground. At the same time, a bull elephant's trunk is strong enough to lift 600 pounds (272 kg) with the help of its tusks. Researchers think the trunk contains 150,000 muscles. You only have about 850 muscles in your entire body.

The elephant's trunk is so good at what it does that a branch of the U.S. military is at work on a robot with a flexible tentacle, called a soft robotic manipulator, that is modeled in part on the amazing elephant trunk.

LEFT: An Asian elephant trunk

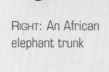

RIGHT: An African elephant trunk

Once researchers knew what kinds of sounds elephants could make, they wanted to know what the sounds meant. They wanted to know what messages were being transmitted to other elephants by particular sounds and how elephants might use sounds differently in different situations. Pairing observation in the wild with new analysis techniques in the lab, scientists began to get an idea of what elephants might be saying with all those roars and rumbles, trumpets and chirps.

DECODING ELEPHANT SOUNDS

Studies on the herds at Amboseli in Kenya showed that African savanna elephants could use ten basic calls in different combinations and in a wide variety of situations. Some were to reinforce relationships between mother and offspring and between siblings, and to reassert authority between the matriarch and lower-ranking females. Calls were used to alert the herd to the approach of unknown elephants, predators, or humans. Matriarchs used calls to stay in touch with the herd and gather them back together. And calls became very important during the rare times that bull elephants encountered a female elephant in heat, ready to mate. Some calls were unique to bulls in musth (a state of sexual high alert in bull elephants), bulls fighting over a female, and females announcing that they were ready to mate.

The most basic way to study elephant communication is by direct observation. Researchers spend long hours in a blind, bunker, or tower. From there they can watch a wild family group and record what individual elephants, both callers and listeners, are doing before and after a vocalization.

But under actual field conditions, direct observation has its limits. Sometimes the animals are too spread out across their territory for the scientist to see which animal is calling or to tell which possible "receivers" are within listening range. Asian elephants and African forest elephants spend most of their time in wooded areas, which may make direct observation difficult or impossible.

Technology offers a way to get around these limitations. Researchers at study sites around the world are using a variety of high-tech approaches to capture calls, identify which elephants are calling, and analyze what the calls mean in the context of herd behavior.

MICROPHONES IN THE TREES

The Cornell Laboratory of Ornithology in Ithaca, New York, developed Autonomous Recording Units, or ARUs, for recording birdsongs. Powered by a truck or lantern battery, the ARU is a small, waterproof unit that records animal vocalizations and other sounds and saves them as digital files on a computer's hard drive. Each unit is also equipped with a Global Positioning System (GPS). The unit records day and night, in any weather, for up to five months before the researcher needs to climb the tree, retrieve the unit, and replace the battery.

Researcher Peter Wredge prepares an Autonomous Recording Unit (ARU). The unit will be hoisted up into a tree in Gabon to record elephant sounds.

African forest elephants at Dzanga Bai of the Central African Republic dig for mud in a forest clearing. This is the site where Andrea Turkalo and Katy Payne recorded elephant sounds for study.

In 1999 Katy Payne of Cornell University organized the Elephant Listening Project (ELP). She wondered whether the ARU technology could help in the collection of data about secretive forest elephants. Payne approached elephant researcher Andrea Turkalo, who had been conducting a long-term study of forest elephants at a site called Dzanga Bai in the Central African Republic.

Bai is the local word for the marshy clearings that dot the dense forest. Elephants visit these clearings to wallow in the mud (which covers their sensitive skin with an all-purpose sunscreen and insect repellent) and to drink the mineral-rich water. Turkalo had been using traditional observation. But she found it was often hard to match the behavior she observed with a corresponding call or to know which animal was calling among the fifty to a hundred animals that could be visiting the bai at any one time.

Working with Turkalo, the ELP team placed seven ARUs around the clearing the forest elephants visited most often. As each elephant called, its vocalization was recorded at all seven ARUs. The sound arrived at each unit a few milliseconds behind or earlier than the others, depending on the distance it traveled from the elephant. By measuring the tiny differences in arrival times, researchers were able to pinpoint the location of the elephant calling. This way they could match vocalizations to specific elephants and eavesdrop on elephant conversations.

Forest elephants appeared to use the same basic calls as savanna elephants, and they used calls to stay in touch when separated in the dense forest. The forest elephants had a particularly rich set of greeting calls and an elaborate greeting ceremony when they reunited with relatives at a clearing.

Back in the lab at Cornell, researchers use a scientific instrument called a sound spectrograph to analyze the vocalizations collected in the field. Originally used to analyze human speech and music, these machines were used in the 1970s to study animal sounds, particularly birdsongs. Older models consisted of an audiotape playback unit, a filter, and a pen or a needle that traced the sound waves on paper. Newer models use computer software. Images produced by spectrographs are called spectrograms.

Research at Dzanga Bai and other sites continues to produce intriguing findings. Forest elephants appear to change the meaning of their calls when they combine them with different gestures, just as humans do. And playback experiments reveal that elephants can identify related elephants by their calls. Matching calls to elephant movements and other behaviors is allowing researchers to put together the beginnings of an "elephant dictionary."

Katy Payne is photographed here in Dzanga Bai in 2000. She will take the recordings gathered here back to her lab at Cornell University in New York.

Dr. Anne Savage, a conservation biologist at Disney's Animal Kingdom, holds up a recording collar designed to monitor the vocalizations produced by elephants.

Technology is also helping to tease apart secrets of elephant communication among captive populations. At the Wildlife Tracking Center at Disney's Animal Kingdom in Florida, researchers Anne Savage and Joe Soltis wanted to know what all the rumbling was about. But the elephants' rumbles were often too soft to be picked up by their microphones. They designed a microphone collar to be fitted on each of the twelve African savanna elephants in the Disney herd. These collars could capture and transmit their vocalizations.

Each elephant's collar transmits on a different frequency. This way, the researchers can tune in to the calls of different individuals and pair them with GPS data about each elephant's movements. This allows the Disney researchers to match the calls to the elephant making them, track elephants as they vocalize and move around the 7-acre (2.9-hectare) exhibit, capture their ongoing social behavior, and monitor their hormonal cycles. Putting these pieces of the puzzle together allows Savage and Soltis to see how vocalizations relate to the way elephants interact with one another and how they reproduce—a vital mission for elephant conservation programs in zoos.

GROWLS, SQUEAKS, AND CHIRPS: ASIAN ELEPHANTS

G. M. McKay first studied the vocalizations of Asian elephants in the early 1970s. McKay described ten different call types in three categories: growls, squeaks, and snorts. Growls included rumbles and roars, and squeaks included chirps and trumpets.

In 2005 German university student Meike Artelt began new research into Asian elephant vocalizations. She was especially interested in the Asian elephant's chirp. Described as a call made up of many short squeaks, the chirp had long been considered unique to the Asian elephant. Over the course of two studies, Artelt recorded seven hundred hours of vocalizations from sixty-four elephants at six zoos across Europe. Analysis revealed that calls differed by age, sex, and situation.

Trumpets were mostly used by adult females when they were excited by something, either in a good or bad way. Calves would frequently trumpet during play. The rumble was used by all, though Artelt thought her captive Asian zoo elephants used it less than wild African savanna elephants. Everyone roared, regardless of age, sex, or status in the herd. Adults roared during incidents of aggression or when they seemed upset about something. Calves roared while begging for milk.

As for that famous Asian elephant chirp, it seems to be unique to adult female elephants. Artelt has yet to record it from a calf or a bull. Artelt thinks Asian elephants may only chirp in certain areas of Asia. Another possibility is that the chirp is used by lower-ranking elephants when calling to higher-ranking elephants. Artelt's research project continues. She thinks there may turn out to be many call variations, even Asian elephant dialects or accents.

BABY ELEPHANTS BABBLE

Angela Stöger-Horwath works at the Mammal Communication Lab at Zoo Vienna in Austria. She wanted to know what calls young elephants made, how and why they used them, and whether there were any differences between old and young calves or between the males and the females. She knew that elephant bulls and cows were quite different in the calls they used. Would the calves show the same differences?

She studied young calves at the zoo in Vienna *(below)* and at an elephant orphanage in Kenya. At these two sites, she recorded twelve hundred calls by eleven elephants, from newborns to eighteen-month-old "toddlers." As it turned out, the male and female calves in the study all babbled more or less the same way, though the males were measurably louder when begging to nurse. They all used the same six calls—rumble, bark, grunt, roar, snort, and trumpet—but the combination of calls they used changed as they grew older.

"Working with elephant toddlers in close proximity is pretty challenging," says Stöger-Horwath, "since they are interested in everything around them, including the observing scientist. However, experiencing the way orphaned calves sought body contact and care was very heartwarming."

Most other work on how young animals acquire a working vocabulary of calls has been done on primates and human babies. Scientists think these babbling elephant calves might shed light on the role imitation plays in the vocal development in a complex society.

During this same period, researcher Smita Nair was studying the calls of a group of wild Asian elephants at a sanctuary in southern India. Nair found four major categories of vocalization: trumpets, chirps, roars, and rumbles. Nair works with Raman Sukumar at the Indian Institute of Science in Bangalore, India. Sukumar is one of the world's leading experts on the Asian elephant. He and his team hope to find ways to use insights into elephant communication and behavior to reduce conflict between humans and elephants.

The more researchers learn about elephant vocalization, the more questions they have. More studies will be needed before we know whether elephants really speak in dialects, have individual accents, or use calls that contradict their body language.

CHAPTER 3

TALKING THROUGH WALLS:
INFRASOUND

How is an elephant like a pipe organ? The elephant research pioneer Katy Payne was able to answer that question in 1984.

When we met her in chapter 2, Payne was already an elephant researcher. But back in 1984, she was a bioacoustician studying the songs of whales. Bioacousticians are scientists who study the sounds animals make and how they use them. When an opportunity arose to record elephant vocalizations in the Oregon Zoo in Portland, Oregon, she took the chance. Payne spent a week at the elephant house, recording the elephants, but she left unsure she'd learned anything significant.

Then on her seat on the plane home, as Payne thought back on the interactions among the zoo's eleven elephants, she found herself wondering about the low rumblings the elephants had made, rumblings she had felt rather than heard.

An elephant stands in a watering hole in the Okavango Delta in Botswana at dusk. Katy Payne studied the many ways elephants use sounds to communicate with one another.

THE SILENT WORLD
OF INFRASOUND

Infrasound is sound that is too low in frequency to be heard by the human ear. A whole branch of science, infrasonics, is devoted to studying these secret sound waves. Earth is a noisy place, once you tune in to infrasound.

Infrasound equipment is used to pick up the low sounds produced by earthquakes, avalanches, volcanoes and, at the very, very low end, the northern lights, or aurora borealis. In the animal kingdom, creatures as diverse as giraffes and hippos, alligators, and tigers are known to produce infrasound calls.

Payne remembered when she was thirteen and singing with a choir in a chapel with an enormous pipe organ. As the organist played, the low notes had dropped out of Payne's range of hearing. As she sang with the other choir members, she had felt the low notes as a throbbing in the air around her.

More than thirty years later, Payne wondered if the two phenomena—the rumblings of the elephants and the shuddering air of the pipe organ—were the same thing. Could the elephants at the Portland Zoo be communicating using sounds below the range of human hearing?

In the fall of 1984, armed with sensitive recording equipment, Payne returned to Portland and began to record the elephants' silent rumbles, matching the vibrations to diaries of their behaviors. Over and over, Payne and her fellow researchers felt throbbing in the air around the elephants, even when the huge animals weren't making any audible sound. The calls were so low they fell into a class of sounds scientists call infrasound.

Back in Payne's lab at Cornell, when the tapes were played back at ten times normal speed through special equipment, the scientists could finally hear for themselves the infrasound calls, "a little like the mooing of cows."

Payne had discovered that elephants use infrasound. "No one who knew elephants was surprised," she later recalled. Iain Douglas-Hamilton, who did groundbreaking work on savanna elephants in Tanzania in the 1960s, once joked that elephants must have ESP—some power of extrasensory perception humans didn't share—that allowed them to find one another over vast distances. In 1972 Indian conservationist and wildlife photographer Madhaviah Krishnan had proposed infrasound as a possible communication channel in elephants, but he did not have the equipment to test his theory. And while Payne and her colleagues were making their first recordings of Asian elephants at the Portland Zoo, researcher Judith Berg was making her own recordings of the elephants at the San Diego Zoo in California. Many researchers had found pieces of the infrasound puzzle. They began to put them in place.

The discovery of infrasound communication in captive elephants seemed to raise as many questions as it answered. Researchers wondered how this method of communication had arisen and why. Did all elephant species use it? Did they use it in the wild? Researchers began to examine the elephant's social structure, environment, and way of life to try to answer these questions.

After Payne published her discovery in a scientific journal, research into this new mode of elephant communication began in earnest. Over the next thirteen years, from 1984 to 1997, researchers confirmed that African savanna elephants use infrasound and began to understand the richness of this mode of communication.

Researchers with the Elephant Listening Project at Cornell found the infrasonic signal often overlapped with a rumble. They examined more than seventeen thousand elephant calls, looking for infrasonic rumbles among the background infrasound produced by wind, thunder, trucks, and airplanes. They searched the spectrograms for distinctive eyebrow-shaped signals on the low end of the spectrum, lasting between two and ten seconds.

They found that most infrasonic calling takes place in family groups and that females appear to use infrasound more often than males. Elephants use infrasonic calls in a variety of ways. These included gathering the herd, coordinating movements, and announcing availability for mating. Elephants also used infrasonic rumbles when competing for food or jockeying for dominance within the herd.

THE ELEPHANT'S SOUNDSCAPE

Why had elephants developed this way of communicating? What good was infrasound in the wild? An examination of the elephant's environment seemed to offer clues. An adult elephant eats 300 to 500 pounds (136 to 227 kg) of food a day, and during the dry season, it can be hard to find. Members of a herd can become separated as they spread out in search of grass and leaves. When foraging among trees and brush, elephants can lose sight of one another.

For years, elephant researchers in the field had been baffled by the sudden coordinated movements of scattered elephant groups. Infrasound appears to offer an explanation for how elephants that have to spread out to forage over a large area can successfully reunite later in the day.

Scientists studying elephants in the wild also wondered how males and females, often separated by great distances, managed to find each other during the short time the female was receptive to mating. Infrasound, able to travel much longer distances than high-frequency calls, seemed to provide an answer.

It turns out that the elephant's sound environment can vary a lot during a single twenty-four-hour period. During the daylight hours in the dry season, wind and temperature keep the elephant's infrasonic calls from traveling much beyond 12 square miles (30 sq. km). In the evening, when temperatures cool, an atmospheric condition called a temperature inversion forms. Cooler air is trapped near the ground, and winds die down. During this inversion, infrasonic waves can travel much farther, covering an area as great as 115 square miles (about 300 sq. km). Researchers have found that elephants' infrasonic calling is at its busiest during the late afternoon and evening hours, when temperature inversions form.

THE EVOLUTION OF INFRASOUND

Michael Garstang of the University of Virginia thinks that infrasound first evolved in the forests where the early elephant ancestors, the proboscideans, evolved. "Very early in their evolution proboscideans developed characteristics that favored [the] generation of low-frequency sounds—long vocal tracts and trunks," he says. "Because . . . such sounds are not weakened by the dense vegetation that covered the continent at the beginning of the Miocene Epoch [a geological period that began 24 million years ago]. The ability to communicate over long distances in such an environment may have been vital to the survival of the first proboscideans."

An elephant herd moves across the savanna at dusk in Botswana's Chobe National Park. Elephants communicate much more during the evenings when infrasonic sound can carry much more easily due to weather conditions.

FLUTTERING FOREHEADS

Researcher Jay Haight at the Oregon Zoo in Portland noticed that an area on an elephant's forehead would flutter when the animal produced low-frequency calls. Researchers found they could use the visible flutter to tell which elephant was issuing an infrasonic call.

Sometimes the call appeared to come from more than one animal. If a calf called out in distress, a general infrasonic rumble might arise from its mothers, aunts, and older sisters. Elephants rumbled infrasonically in response to the researchers departing for the day. A male and a female elephant appeared to converse via infrasound through the wall that separated their enclosures.

Researchers noticed that the skin on elephants' foreheads fluttered when they were making infrasonic calls.

These elephant ancestors probably relied on smell and hearing more than sight to make their way through thick woodlands and stay in touch with one another. By the time forests were replaced by savannas, the elephant's basic body features and senses were already in place. So the ancestor of the savanna elephant emerged onto the grasslands able to communicate at long-range low frequencies. Garstang hopes ongoing research will lead to a more complete view of how elephants use all their senses to function in the herd.

PUTTING THE PIECES TOGETHER

The combined efforts of teams working all around the world are leading to a better understanding of what individual vocalizations and infrasound rumbles mean. So far, scientists have grouped African elephant calls into three categories: those that signal an elephant's hormonal state (readiness to mate); those that advertise excitement, fear, or surprise; and those that help the scattered extended family regroup and stay together in the large and varied landscape of the herd's range.

There is still much to learn. Calls appear to change their meaning when they are paired with other calls, almost like compound words (think of the difference between *cup*, *board*, and *cupboard*). And like many highly social, intelligent animals (including humans), what elephants have to say often depends on which elephants they are talking to. Intriguing observations suggest elephants can tailor their calls, depending on their social rank, whether they are close or distant relatives, and other factors that researchers still have to identify.

CHAPTER 4

EAR FLAPS,
TRUNK CURLS, AND
ELEPHANT
PERFUME

Visual signals are everywhere in the animal kingdom, from a firefly flashing to a peacock spreading its magnificent tail. Some visual signals are easy for us to read. If you see a dog crouched down, with its hind end up and tail wagging furiously, you know it wants to play. Just as clearly, a cat with an arched back and flattened ears doesn't. Many animals use postures to square off with a rival, seem larger to a predator, or advertise to a potential mate.

Since the early 1990s, researchers working with African savanna elephants have been recording the rich vocabulary of body language in elephants. Some messages appear intended for members of the family, others for individuals outside the herd, and still others for different species—including people.

Phil Kahl and Billie Armstrong went to Zimbabwe between 1991 and 1997 to compile a complete list of elephant gestures. They found a particularly varied vocabulary of gestures used by bull elephants in musth.

Elephants use gestures as well as vocalizations to communicate with one another. This elephant curls back its trunk. Do you know what it means? It is often a signal to put a lower-ranking elephant in its place.

A bull elephant during musth swaggers around the watering hole. His rear legs are wet with urine. This all means that he is ready to find a mate.

There was the exaggerated swagger, or musth walk, in which the male struts with head held high. He might also perform gestures like the trunk curl, head toss, or trunk bounce. Kahl and Armstrong also observed bulls in musth wrinkling their trunks, waving their ears, dribbling urine, and marking territory—all considered forms of elephant gestures. For her part, a female in estrus, or heat, would perform an estrus walk, circling the perimeter of the herd and looking back over her shoulder.

In 2004 Kahl, Armstrong, and other elephant researchers began to share and compare their data. Everyone had been calling the various gestures by different names, so the first step was to agree on terms. Then the data were entered into a gestures image database available online. The database at ElephantVoices.org lists 205 gestures in thirty different categories. They range from gestures used to comfort and solicit play, to gestures to bond with herd mates or manage personal space, gestures to guard a mate, or gestures to investigate the body of a herd mate. Scientists anywhere can pull up the image of an elephant gesture and benefit from the knowledge of other researchers about how and when it's used.

TRUNK WRESTLING AND TAIL SLAPS

Elephants use infrasound to stay in touch over vast distances, but when they are closer together—within a trunk's length—they get their point across with touch. The elephant "handshake" consists of one elephant inserting the tip of its trunk into the mouth of a family member. Two elephants will also twine their trunks together upon meeting. In less friendly encounters, trunk wrestling contests take place between males. Female elephants can discipline a calf with a trunk slap. A slap can hurt! An elephant's trunk can weigh 300 pounds (135 kg).

Elephants rely on touch in a wide variety of social encounters, both friendly and unfriendly. Mothers and aunts touch their calves to comfort and to discipline them. They nudge them with their tusks to tell them to move along.

Two male Asian elephants greet each other by putting their trunks in each other's mouths.

Elephant calves bump heads in the mud during play. Play fighting helps them find their status among the herd.

Calves use contact to form and maintain bonds with other members of the family. Calves press the legs or breasts of their mothers to beg for milk. (They may even do this with their aunts or older sisters.) Calves also use touch to begin play, almost as if saying, "Tag. You're it!"

Just how elephants use touch can depend on their status within the herd. Allies may click tusks together when meeting as a form of greeting. Elephants of the same rank will stand close together, their sides touching, but a lower-ranking elephant may back up to a higher-ranking one and expose only its less vulnerable rear.

In the mid-1990s, researchers Bets Rasmussen and Bryce Munger had a rare chance to learn more about the amazingly sensitive sense of touch in the elephant's "finger"—the fleshy tip of its trunk. A male Asian elephant in a zoo lost the tip of his trunk in an accident. Rasmussen and Munger were able to analyze the severed finger tissue.

QUIZ: ELEPHANT BODY LANGUAGE

Try to match the gesture with its meaning. Then look at the key to see how well you did. (Some gestures may have more than one correct match.) Turn the page to see the answers.

GESTURE

1) Tossing dust or debris

2) Running with tail straight out behind

3) Trunk curled up in front of face like a party blower

4) Tip of trunk inserted in another elephant's mouth

5) Tail swat to the elephant walking behind

6) High-stepping swagger walk

7) Ear flap

8) Floppy run, tail curled, shaking head side to side

(9) Head tucked below shoulders

MEANING

a) I'm big and bad and looking for a mate.

b) Stop tailgating.

c) Lions! Run away!

d) Hello, friend.

e) Maybe that bigger bull won't notice me.

f) I'm upset.

g) Listen up! We're moving out.

h) I outrank you!

i) Let's play.

Quiz Answers

1-f and i. Elephants often toss debris when agitated, but young calves will also throw sticks or dust during play.

2-c. A tail struck straight out behind usually indicates a high state of surprise and fear.

3-h. A curled-up trunk can mean many things, but when rolled up and unfurled like a party blower, it's usually used to put a subordinate (lower-ranking) herd member in her place.

4-d. Elephants often place the tip of the trunk into the mouth of another elephant in a gesture almost like a human handshake. This greeting often is used when members of a herd reunite after a separation or by a lower-ranking male to greet a dominant male.

5-b. A tail swat tells the elephant behind to back off. An elephant may also use its tail to feel what's behind it.

6-a. This is known to researchers as the musth walk, used by mature bulls in musth to advertise their reproductive prowess to both potential mates and rivals.

7-g. Elephants flap, slap, and wave their ears for a lot of reasons—to cool themselves and to shoo away flies as well as to communicate. This particular kind of ear slap is used by matriarchs to get the herd's attention.

8-i. Calves and other juvenile elephants use this bouncy run and head wagging to say they are ready for play.

9-e. Young bulls may use this head-low posture, with ears folded close to the head, to appear smaller when they are around an older bull in musth.

A dissecting microscope revealed that the tissue of the trunk tip was rich in Pacinian corpuscles, a special type of cell. Under the microscope, Pacinian corpuscles appear layered, like an onion, with the layers separated by a gel. These cells seem to play a role in the sense of touch. The Pacinian corpuscles may make the elephant's trunk tip as sensitive as the tip of a human finger. They may use their finger to read information in their environment the way a sight-impaired person might use their fingers to read braille.

The trunk tip is surrounded by whiskers—the scientific name for them is *vibrissae*. The tip itself is well supplied with vellus vibrissae—tiny, whiskerlike structures just below the surface of the skin. Animals with more prominent whiskers—such as mice and rats—use them to learn about their environment. Scientists are just beginning to learn how the vibrissae in an elephant's trunk might help it detect signals to interpret the world around it.

The tip of an elephant's trunk is very sensitive and is surrounded by vibrissae, or whiskers.

"HOVERING AND WHIFFLING"

In her memoir, *Silent Thunder*, elephant researcher Katy Payne describes the way a group of elephants checked her out by sampling her human scent with their trunks:

> Rosy was granting her herd the privilege of exploring my smell carefully. . . . She growled when a calf became too inquisitive, and the little trunk hastily withdrew. . . . I wished that I had a hovering and whiffling trunk of my own so I could learn the same things about the elephants that they were learning about me.

What are elephants able to learn with their hovering, whiffling trunks? We know that elephants have an excellent sense of smell. Turbinates are structures in the nose that help mammals smell. Elephants have more turbinates than any other animal, even dogs. These structures hang down in

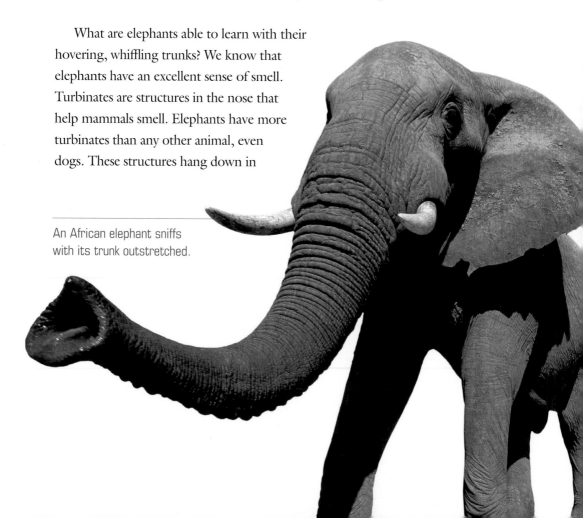

An African elephant sniffs with its trunk outstretched.

folds, like the leaves of a book, in the front of the elephant's skull. They give the elephant a total smelling surface area equivalent to a small throw rug. (In contrast, we humans have an area for smelling the size of two postage stamps.) This large smelling surface gives elephants the ability to smell a watering hole from several miles away. Scientists are learning more about how elephants use that sense of smell to recognize relatives, find mates, and detect predators.

Elephants can often be seen touching the tip of the trunk to a spot on the ground or to some part of a herd mate's anatomy— sometimes the genitals or sometimes a gland between the eye and ear called the temporal gland. (During musth, the temporal glands of bull elephants exude a smelly secretion.) The elephant will then touch the tip of its trunk, containing the sample, to the roof of its mouth, where there

After touching the ground where a female elephant has urinated, this male Asian elephant touches its trunk to the roof of its mouth. A special organ there gives the elephant information about the female's mating status.

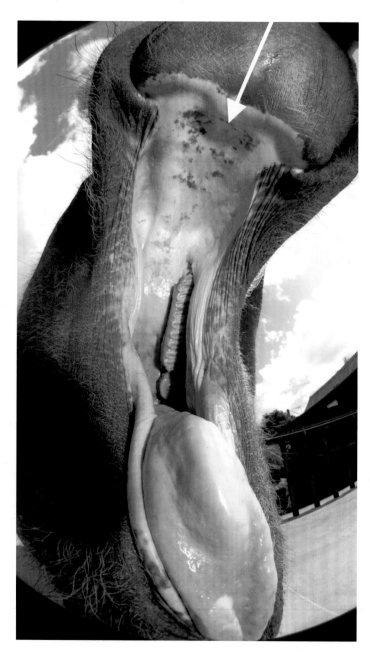

are openings to two small, straw-shaped tubes. These are a special sense organ known as the vomeronasal organ (VNO). By sampling urine or feces on the ground or secretions from another elephant's mouth, temporal gland, or genitals, elephants can learn the reproductive status of another elephant. Chemicals called pheromones communicate this message, which is vital for the survival of the herd.

The arrow in this close-up of the roof of an elephant's mouth points to the sensory organ called the vomeronasal organ (VNO). When the elephant touches the tip of its trunk to the roof of its mouth, it can sense many things about its fellow elephants.

DR. JACOBSON'S ORGAN

In 1813 a Danish surgeon named Ludwig Lewin Jacobson discovered the Jacobson's organ—the structure in the human nose later named after him. It was somewhat ironic that Jacobson's organ (also known as the vomeronasal organ, or VNO) was discovered first in people. It is an organ that is put to much better use in other mammals, notably cats, large and small, and the ungulates (a big family of large-toed mammals including horses, bison, camels, and tapirs, among others). It's also a sensory organ found in snakes and some lizards.

You may have seen a cat curl back its lip and gape slightly while smelling something interesting. This is a behavior known as the flehmen response, from a German word for curling the lip. The cat is drawing odors to the roof of its mouth, where they enter its Jacobson's organ.

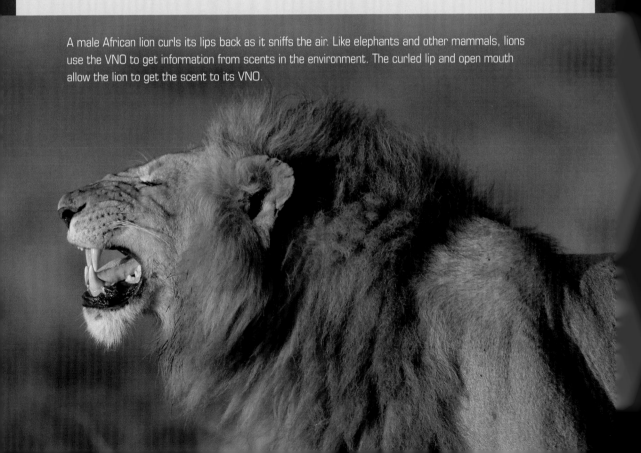

A male African lion curls its lips back as it sniffs the air. Like elephants and other mammals, lions use the VNO to get information from scents in the environment. The curled lip and open mouth allow the lion to get the scent to its VNO.

SEEING RED AND
SMELLING DANGER

Elephants use visual and chemical cues to keep track of predators in their environment—even when those predators are people. In a study conducted in Kenya in 2007, researchers found that elephants could tell apart men from two different ethnic groups. The first group were men from the Kamba clan of farmers, who posed no threat to them. In the second group were men from the Maasai tribe *(left)*, nomadic herders who are known to spear elephants. When researchers presented elephants with clothing worn by Maasai tribesmen, they reacted with a display of fear. The elephants also reacted fearfully to the red color associated with the Maasai's traditional robes. The clothes worn by the Kamba farmers got a much milder reaction. The elephants apparently can tell the difference between the two groups of men based on subtle chemical cues left on the cloth, the same kinds of clues bloodhounds use when tracking lost or missing people.

AN ANCIENT CHEMICAL LANGUAGE

Pheromones are chemicals secreted by animals to signal to members of the same or another species. They may serve a number of very different functions: attracting potential mates, for instance, or warning the herd to gather or disperse under threat of a predator. Animals use pheromones to mark territory. A dog lifting his leg to urinate on a tree is letting other dogs know he's been there. A cat rubbing her head on the furniture is also leaving her scent.

Scientists who study the ways chemical messages influence animals in their environment are called chemical ecologists. Chemical ecologists have only really begun to study chemical messaging in depth over the last thirty-five years, using sophisticated new lab equipment. They have learned a lot about the chemical ecology of insects, especially in ants, bees, and moths. They are just beginning to study the chemical language in other animals, including mammals such as elephants.

Elephants release pheromones in their urine, on their breath, and from the temporal gland. Secretions from the temporal gland appear to be an important way for mature bull elephants to signal that they are in musth.

Secretions from the temporal glands of these older bull elephants in musth contain high levels of a pheromone called frontalin. Research by Bets Rasmussen, David Greenwood, and their colleagues showed that immature bulls produced a substance with a honeylike odor from their temporal gland. When Rasmussen analyzed the secretion in her lab at Oregon Health and Science University, she discovered that the frontalin molecule in the elephants came in two forms. The ratio of one form of frontalin to the other form seems to make the difference between the stinky temporal secretions of a mature bull in musth and the sweeter-smelling secretions of an immature bull. Rasmussen and her colleagues wondered whether the message the young bulls were sending to the older males was this: don't worry—I'm not competing with you.

Experiments in 2007 by researcher Lucy Bates show that elephants may use chemical cues to keep tabs on absent herd mates. Female elephants at Amboseli

Chemical secretions from this elephant's temporal gland let others know he is in musth.

National Park showed the most interest in urine-soaked earth samples when the urine was from a female family member who wasn't present or from an elephant that was walking behind them and could not have deposited fresh urine. They showed less interest in the fresh urine of elephants that were not related to them or that were walking ahead of them. The experiment suggests that elephants are able to keep a mental tally of who is present or absent and who is ahead or behind them in line. The cues in the odors may help elephants form a chemical mental map of their social network.

HOW DO YOU COLLECT
ELEPHANT-TRUNK MUCUS?

F irst, get your elephant to hold its trunk up for two minutes. Then get it to blow into a plastic bag. You will collect about 50 milliliters (3.3 tablespoons) of goo.

Collecting mucus from the vomeronasal organ ducts in the roof of an elephant's mouth is trickier and demands a steady hand. Bets Rasmussen and David Greenwood used a baby feeding catheter (a narrow tube used in hospitals to feed tiny premature babies).

"The procedure [shown at right] involved inserting the tube very carefully several centimeters into the VNO duct, using suction from a syringe to draw the mucus up through the catheter. We might get 10 to 30 ml [2 to 6 teaspoons] if we're lucky," says Greenwood. While attempting this very tricky maneuver, Rasmussen and Greenwood might occasionally come in contact with the elephant's tongue, which is soft, smooth, and surprisingly ticklish.

He explains they are looking for proteins in the hard-won sample of mucus. Researchers believe these proteins bind with pheromones and carry them up the elephant's VNO duct to the vomeronasal organ itself. Once there, olfactory receptors (nerve cells that detect odors) relay the message to a part of the brain that can decode the pheromone's code. Greenwood believes the proteins in both trunk and VNO mucus play a crucial role in getting information about potential mates to the elephant's brain, helping elephants find mates.

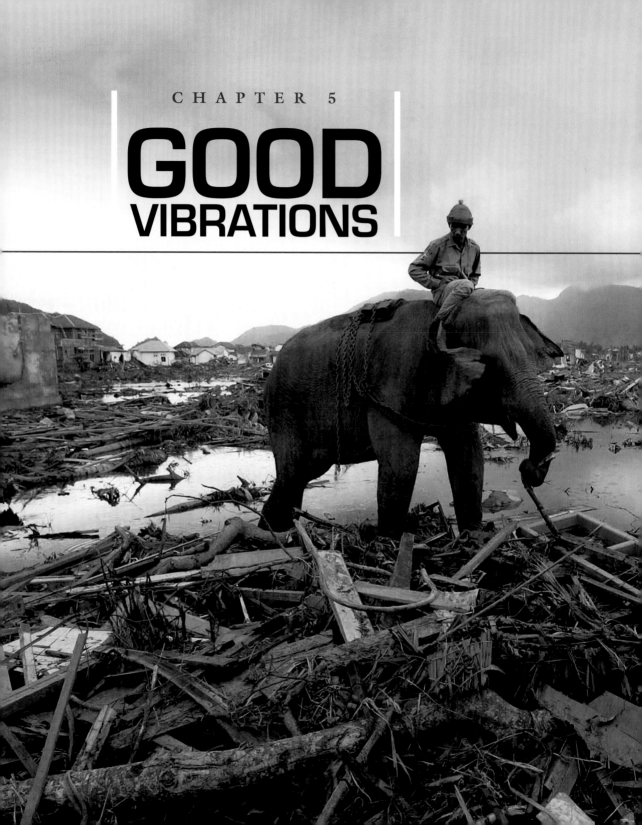

CHAPTER 5

GOOD
VIBRATIONS

On December 26, 2004, an underwater earthquake off the coast of Sumatra, an island of Indonesia, sent a series of deadly tsunamis (tidal waves) racing to the shores surrounding the Indian Ocean. Amid the destruction and terrible loss of life came reports of an amazing phenomenon. Survivors in Thailand and Sri Lanka told of elephants fleeing to higher ground in the moments before the tidal waves struck.

Back in the United States, the phone began to ring at the office of researcher Peggy Hill, a biology professor at the University of Tulsa in Tulsa, Oklahoma. Hill is an expert in the use of vibrations as a means of communication in animals. The reporters wanted to know whether elephants have some sixth sense that gave them advance warning of the approaching disaster.

The answer Hill gave them was maybe. It's hard for science to explain why animals behave strangely before storms and other

Elephants were some of the first animals to flee low-lying areas before the 2004 tsunami struck coastlines in Southeast Asia. This Asian elephant helps clean up some of the debris left in the wake of the tsunami's destruction in Indonesia.

natural disasters. Scientists do know that events such as underwater earthquakes create Rayleigh waves. These are vibrations that arrive hours before a tsunami itself. And they know that many creatures can sense Rayleigh waves.

Vibration is an ancient means of communication, one of the earliest to evolve in the animal kingdom. It is used by a remarkable range of animals from snakes and scorpions to naked mole rats and elephants.

In July 2004, elephant researcher Caitlin O'Connell-Rodwell camped out at a watering hole at the Etosha National Park in northern Namibia, Africa. She brought a team of experts in geophysics (the study of Earth physics), acoustics (the science of sound), elephant care, and animal medicine, as well as some unusual equipment.

Along with standard audio and video equipment, she had brought along geophones, special devices for detecting seismic vibrations, or vibrations in the ground. Geophones were first used by the military during the Vietnam War (1957–1975) to detect the vibrations of enemy troop movements. O'Connell-Rodwell was hoping to confirm something that she had come to suspect through her previous seven years of research at the Etosha site: the elephants were sending signals as vibrations and sensing vibrations through their feet.

ELEPHANTS ON TIPTOE

O'Connell-Rodwell had become interested in two elephant behaviors she had observed among the herd at Etosha in 1992. The first was something called synchronized freezing, when two or more elephants would suddenly stop and stand stock-still, perhaps while one elephant placed its trunk on the ground. The second behavior that had aroused her curiosity was what she called tiptoeing. Elephants would stop, lean forward with the toes of one front foot on the ground. O'Connell-Rodwell wondered whether the elephants could possibly be sensing vibrations through their feet.

When elephants rumble, these very low calls begin in the elephant's larynx. They are amplified in the special pouch behind the tongue and in the elephant's skull and trunk. Some of the energy from the rumble appears to pass into the ground through

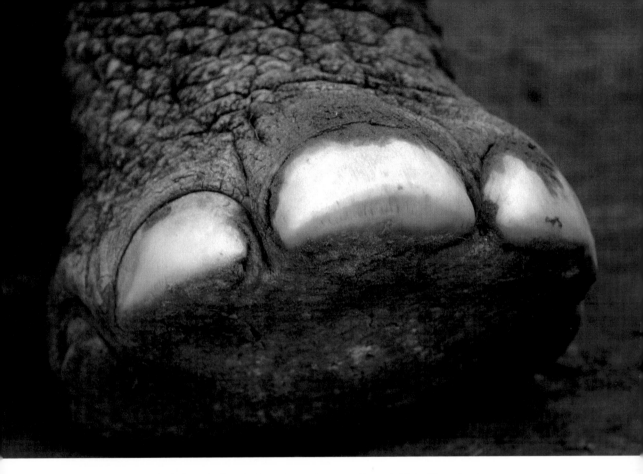

A close look at this Asian elephant's foot shows its toenails and thick-skinned sole. Elephants sense very low sounds through the vibrations they feel through their feet.

the elephant's feet. O'Connell-Rodwell thought that the rumble signal might be picked up by elephants many kilometers away, because these low rumbles have the potential to travel much farther through the ground than through the air.

She relayed her suspicion to her former professor, Lynette Hart of the University of California at Davis, and Hart knew just who to call. Her brother, Byron Arnason, was a geophysicist who specialized in using geophones to pick up vibrations underground. Initial studies with captive elephants in Texas proved the geophones could work. So O'Connell-Rodwell and her colleagues headed into the field to test the equipment on a group of wild elephants.

A WHOLE LOTTA SHAKIN' GOIN' ON

In 2005, when elephant researcher Caitlin O'Connell-Rodwell was planning her next experiment, she went shopping for equipment in an unusual place—a home-theater store. She had already tried using base shakers—devices used in car stereos to add a powerful boom to the bass through the car seats. But she decided she needed something even more powerful.

She found it in a 10-pound (4.5 kg) device made to deliver earthshaking effects to home theaters. It claimed to transfer low-frequency audio directly into the listener's body. O'Connell-Rodwell wondered whether the device might succeed in transferring low-frequency waves directly into an elephant's foot.

Donna the Elephant shakes hands with Colleen Kinzley, an animal curator at the Oakland Zoo in California. Donna participated in experimental trials involving low-frequency soundwaves and vibrations.

O'Connell-Rodwell was working with Donna, a twenty-one-year-old African savanna elephant in the Oakland Zoo in Oakland, California. In the experiment, O'Connell-Rodwell buried a pair of the devices about 20 yards (18 m) from where Donna stood. She played an elephant rumble through them.

Donna had previously been trained to lift her foot in response to an audible rumble. Each time she correctly lifted her foot in response to a rumble, Donna was rewarded with a horse cookie—a favorite treat made of hay and molasses. Since the rumble was no longer audible, would she still detect it through the ground?

She did. Donna responded to the inaudible rumble through the ground just the way she had responded to the audible rumble played through the air. In later experiments, O'Connell-Rodwell rigged a metal platform to deliver a vibration. Then she trained Donna to stand on the metal platform and touch a square metal target with her trunk if she felt a vibration and touch a triangle if she felt nothing. The metal platform could measure precisely how sensitive Donna's foot pads were to vibrations.

Donna the elephant is still taking part in the studies. She looks forward to them so much she starts to salivate when she sees O'Connell-Rodwell approaching with the equipment—and the horse treats!

Donna, standing with her feet on the vibration platform, reaches for the metal target.

The researchers used the geophones to record the elephants' vibrations, carefully making a record of what the animals were doing before, during, and after the vibration. Then they played the vibration back through the ground and watched what happened.

For a month at the height of the scorching dry season, the team remained at the watering hole. A 20-foot (6 m) tower of wood and canvas became their high-tech, solar-powered headquarters. From it they monitored the elephants around the clock as they came to the watering hole to bathe and drink. Combining their observations with the geophone data, O'Connell-Rodwell and her colleagues concluded that elephants were indeed sending and receiving seismic signals through the ground.

THE SECRET OF THE ELEPHANT'S FOOT

Elephants can receive seismic signals in two ways. The first way is through their bones. The elephant stands on tiptoe, and the seismic vibration is carried from the toe bone up the leg to the inner ear. The second way is through the soft pad of the elephant's foot. The fatty cushion of an elephant's foot has a layer rich in Pacinian corpuscles. The fat itself is similar to the special acoustic fat found in the heads of dolphins that helps them focus the beam of sound they use to navigate and locate food. Signals from the elephant's foot travel through nerves to the elephant's brain.

Most mammals have a cochlea—a structure in the inner ear that is tightly coiled like a snail's shell. Biologists had long thought that the cochlea's snail shape was so that it could fit in a small space inside the skull. They often unrolled dissected cochleas in the lab to study them. But in the 1980s, a neurologist suggested that the coiling served a different purpose. He examined the inner ears of several ground-dwelling mammals and concluded that the number of coils in the cochlea was related to the ability to hear very low frequencies and vibrations. The elephant's cochlea seems to be one of the most finely tuned in the animal kingdom.

UMBRELLA STAND OR SOPHISTICATED LISTENING DEVICE?

At the height of safari hunting in the late nineteenth century, a strange and grisly souvenir could be found in the parlors of some homes. Gentlemen often stored their walking sticks and umbrellas in a preserved elephant's foot. Elephants' feet that were once just umbrella stands are being given new attention by modern science.

Researchers have discovered that the elephant's foot is constructed not just to bear the animal's great weight. The fatty pads on each foot are sensitive to pressure and pain. They can even detect seismic waves through the ground.

These elephant feet were turned into stools and plant stands.

THE TELEPHONE ENGINEER AND THE ELEPHANT'S EARS

In 1928 Hungarian Georg von Békésy, a physicist and anatomist, was working to design a better telephone earphone. This is the part of the old-fashioned telephone receiver that people held up to their ears. He devised a model of the human cochlea, or inner ear, by filling a metal tube with water and stretching a membrane over a narrow window in the tube. He was able to study how sound waves behaved as they traveled through the fluid. Békésy dissected the inner ears of human cadavers and animals under the microscope, using tiny tools he made himself. He concluded that high sounds were perceived at the base of the coil and low sounds were perceived at its center.

Békésy was eager to study the cochlea of any animal that came his way. In the 1940s, he heard that an elephant in the Budapest Zoo in Hungary had died. He went to the zoo to ask for the ears, but he learned that the elephant's carcass had already been shipped to a glue factory. Békésy sent his assistant to get the inner ears. To his dismay, his assistant returned dragging the large outer ears down the hallway! Békésy hurried to the factory and was able to retrieve the precious cochleas for study before they were turned into glue.

His experiments won him the Nobel Prize for Physiology or Medicine in 1961. His work is still cited by researchers looking into the secrets of animal hearing.

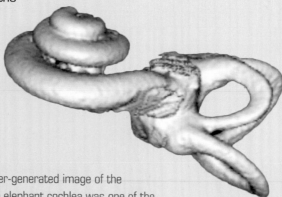

This is a three-dimensional computer-generated image of the cochlea from an Asian elephant. The elephant cochlea was one of the inner ear structures Georg von Békésy used in his study of sound in the 1940s.

Research shows that African savanna elephants are able to sense subtle differences among seismic calls made in the similar situations. They go on high alert when they feel a herd mate's alarm rumble, but not when they hear a nearly identical rumble from an elephant not in the same group. O'Connell-Rodwell thinks it may be that the herd mate's alarm has more meaning, and this prompts a strong response. Another possibility, she thinks, is that elephants may not consider alarm calls from strangers to be trustworthy.

The ability to communicate with other herds through this seismic channel may offer elephants several advantages. Staying in touch with other herds over long distances may help reduce competition over watering holes or food sources. It may allow elephants to share information about the location of predators and keep tabs on potential mates.

Insights into elephant communication may yield benefits for human health. O'Connell-Rodwell's research into seismic communication in elephants may help doctors create devices and therapies to help hard-of-hearing children learn to listen through vibrations.

CHAPTER 6

GODS AND MONSTERS:
THE ELEPHANT-
HUMAN
RELATIONSHIP

It was late August in Hyderabad, India, just before the start of the festival of Ganesh. Some students from the local schools had set up a table outdoors and covered it with little clay figures of the Hindu elephant-headed god, Ganesh. The students and their teachers held signs saying "SAVE THE EARTH" and "SAVE THE ENVIRONMENT." But the most attention-getting sight at the rally was the students who, stripped to the waist, were wearing Ganesh's traditional costume and homemade elephant masks.

The students were trying to get people to change the way they celebrated Ganesh's birthday. Members of the Hindu faith revere Ganesh and consider him the god of wisdom and prosperity and the remover of obstacles. During his ten-day birthday celebration, called Ganesh Chaturthi, images of the elephant-headed deity can be found everywhere throughout India, from private homes to public street corners. As the festival nears its end, huge crowds gather to carry towering plaster-of-Paris images of Ganesh to the edge of the local waterway. Immersing the idols in the sea or another body of water is an important part of the ritual.

To celebrate the birth of Hindu god Ganesh, crowds of Hindus in Mumbai, India, tow plaster statues of the elephant god into the Arabian Sea. Throughout India, giant idols of Ganesh are immersed in rivers, lakes, and the ocean during the festival.

But these colorful images of Ganesh are an ecological nightmare. The plaster of Paris slowly dissolves in water, releasing gypsum, sulfur, phosphorus, and magnesium. The colorful paints that decorate the statues are even more toxic, releasing lead, cadmium, and mercury—the same heavy metals found in batteries.

Recently, ecology-minded school students from the Indian cities of Mumbai, Hyderabad, Mysore, and Bangalore have been organizing campaigns for a greener Ganesh festival, urging Hindus to immerse a reusable brass image of the god or one made of clay or other natural materials. With its mix of reverence and destruction, tradition clashing with the realities of the twenty-first century, the Ganesh festival can be seen as a parable for the long, complex, and often troubled relationship between humans and elephants.

In 2009 in parts of India, schoolchildren dressed as the Hindu god Ganesh to protest the use of plaster figurines decorated with toxic paints. Left in local waterways at the end of the festival, the figurines dissolve, and the plaster and paint pollute the water.

MOHENJO-DARO

The story begins in the remains of an ancient city on the bank of the Indus River, in what is modern southern Pakistan. The Indus Valley Civilization flourished here between 2600 and 1900 B.C.

Traces of the Indus Valley Civilization remain in the form of several mud-brick cities, including Mohenjo-daro. Elephant bones have been excavated here, as well as clay seals that show elephants that appear to be wearing blankets or cloths, as though they were used to carry loads. Elephants may have been hunted

for meat and ivory in this region five thousand years ago. But evidence at Mohenjo-daro and other sites suggests that even then, people began to see elephants as intelligent and obedient creatures, whose great strength could be put to use. It was here in southern Pakistan that the human-elephant relationship began to change.

LEFT: This seal depicting an elephant was found at the site of Mohenjo-daro (BELOW), the ancient city of the Indus Valley Civilization that thrived more than four thousand years ago in what is now Pakistan.

P. T. Barnum of Barnum & Bailey Circus purchased Jumbo (ABOVE) from the London Zoo in 1882. Animal rights groups claim that modern-day circuses mistreat elephants and use harsh methods to train them. In 2009 an animal rights group sued Ringling Brothers and Barnum & Bailey Circus, arguing that the circus's treatment of animals was cruel.

Over the next six thousand years, elephants were used as beasts of burden, worshipped in temples, and trained to work in logging camps and circuses. In India, war elephants were even used to lead the charge into battle, serving as living armored personnel carriers. Elephants were valued for their intelligence, strength, and great size. But the human-elephant relationship was also shaped by the value of the elephant's ivory tusks.

Smooth, white ivory could be carved into intricate designs, and since ancient times, it had been prized as a raw material for works of art and luxury items for royalty. For centuries ivory was carved by hand. Then in the early 1800s, inventors devised machinery to mass-produce ivory objects, and hunters moved into the interior of Africa to satisfy the demand for the raw material. Ivory was used to make so many objects in the nineteenth century—from billiard balls and piano keys to dominoes and ladies' sewing kits—that writer John Frederick Walker calls ivory "the plastic of its age."

GOING, GOING, GONE?

At the beginning of the nineteenth century, scientists think there may still have been 27 million elephants left in Africa. Between 1860 and 1930, from 25,000 to 100,000 elephants were killed each year for their ivory. In the 1950s, after some national parks were established in Africa, elephants' numbers recovered a little, and several million were still left by the end of the 1960s. But in the 1970s, the price of ivory increased tenfold. Elephants were killed by the thousands to satisfy a new market for ivory. Numbers plun ͮed from 1.3 million in 1979 to fewer than 600,000 a decade later.

Laws were passed to protect elep'   ˙e sale of ivory, but the laws contributed to a new, unofficial '   ͮ. The African Elephant

The decaying bodies fror͢   ˢ can be seen in this 2004 photograph taken over Tsavo Easˈ   These elephants were killed by poachers for their tusks alone. The͢   ˌ were left to rot.

Japanese customs officials tag nearly 3 tons (2.7 metric tons) of black-market ivory elephant tusks that were confiscated from smugglers in Osaka, Japan, in 2007.

Status Report for 2007 estimated the total wild population of elephants in Africa at between 420,000 and 690,000. Poaching continues partly because of desperate poverty, particularly in Africa, and an ongoing demand for ivory in Southeast Asia. Well-to-do Japanese, Thai, and Chinese businesspeople continue to present ivory gifts to mark special occasions and to make business deals. There is also a market for illegal ivory in the United States, where ivory is prized for gun grips and knife handles. If poaching continues at current rates, some experts think elephants could be extinct in the wild by 2025.

The ivory ban remains in place, but conservationists don't agree on whether it is working. Some feel that elephants can only be saved by helping the people who live alongside elephants see the animals' value as living creatures.

HOW WILL WE ANSWER THE ELEPHANTS' CALL?

In 2009 the Central Zoo Authority in India made headlines when it declared that all captive elephants in Indian zoos were to be moved to sanctuaries or wildlife parks. Four years earlier, the Detroit Zoo in Detroit, Michigan, had sent its elephants to a wildlife sanctuary in California, and at least five other zoos have decided to close their elephant exhibits after their aging animals die. Activists are lobbying smaller zoos in northern states or with small, outdated elephant enclosures to move their elephants to elephant sanctuaries in warmer parts of the country, closer to the climate of their natural habitats.

At the same time, forty other U.S. zoos had plans to enlarge or renovate their elephant enclosures. They are saying that elephants in zoos benefit both elephants and people. Zoo-based research and public education both contribute to conservation, these zoos argue.

Felix, a female African elephant at the Maryland Zoo in Baltimore, savors a pumpkin. In a practice called enrichment, zookeepers provide animals with treats like pumpkins and toys like barrels and tires to challenge them mentally and relieve boredom.

TIMELINE

This timeline shows some of the shared history of humans and elephants.

9,000 B.C. Prehistoric people living in present-day Mutoko, Zimbabwe, leave paintings on a cave wall showing an elephant hunt.

3,000 B.C. Clay seals from the Indus Valley of modern Pakistan have images of tamed elephants.

218 B.C. Hannibal, an African general, fights the Roman army using forty thousand soldiers and thirty-seven battle elephants.

CA. A.D. 400 Ganesh, the elephant-headed god, emerges as a distinct deity in the Hindu pantheon.

796 The caliph (Islamic spiritual leader) of Baghdad, in Iraq, presents Charlemagne, ruler of most of Europe, with the gift of an elephant.

1779 A machine to make hair combs from elephant ivory is patented, leading to the mass production of ivory objects, from piano keys to billiard balls.

1796 Sea captain Jacob Crowninshield displays a two-year-old female Asian elephant on Broadway in New York City.

1874 An editorial cartoon by Thomas Nast in *Harper's Magazine* marks the first use of an elephant as a symbol of the Republican Party in the United States.

1880 The first baby elephant is born in the United States and is named Columbia.

1941 Walt Disney releases the feature animated film, *Dumbo*, about a young flying elephant.

1965 Iain and Oria Douglas-Hamilton begin a forty-year field study of elephants in Tanzania.

1989 The African elephant is added to the international list of endangered species, with an estimated six hundred thousand individuals remaining in the wild.

2009 Researchers sequence the African elephant's DNA.

2010 In Doha, Qatar, representatives from governments around the world vote down a proposal to weaken a twenty-one-year-old ban on the ivory trade.

The debate continues: if captured elephants don't belong in zoos, where do they belong? Wild elephant populations are being squeezed into ever smaller spaces by expanding human populations, and they are under threat from poaching.

So where do elephants belong? There is no single answer and no agreement among those who study elephants in the wild and those committed to zoo-based conservation and captive breeding. But one possible answer may lie in making life better for both wild and captive elephants—as well as the people who live alongside them in their natural ranges. The knowledge scientists have gained about elephant societies and elephant communication can help both efforts.

MAKING LIFE BETTER FOR WORKING ELEPHANTS

One-third of Asian elephants live in captivity as working elephants in logging and tourism. Traditional methods of elephant handling relied on a philosophy of human dominance and a sharp elephant hook. But some dedicated elephant advocates in Nepal are working to change that.

In 1995 Helena Telkanranta of World Wildlife Fund (WWF) Finland proposed to Chandra Gurung at WWF–Nepal that they find a solution to the often brutal methods used by mahouts (elephant handlers) to train elephants. They invited Western animal-training experts to hold a workshop for Nepalese mahouts to teach them gentler training methods. The first workshop was in Chitwan, Nepal, in 2006. The Working Elephant Programme of Asia was founded in 2008 to keep the workshops going. The work is continued under an organization named Human Elephant Learning Programs.

At the Elephant Breeding Centre at Bardia National Park in Nepal, four young elephants and their mahouts are taking part in a pilot project to try out the new training methods, substituting rewards and repetition for the elephant hook. Depending on the results, the Nepalese government may adopt new regulations mandating more humane methods to train elephants in the whole country.

"This method is so much friendlier to the elephants," says Chandra Man Tamang, head of the Elephant Breeding Centre and a veteran trainer. "They also learn quicker this way. For me, there is no going back to the old method."

"WE RIDE YOU AS AN ELEPHANT, BUT WE KNOW YOU ARE A GOD"

PROFILE: Satya Narayan, elephant handler, Chitwan, Nepal

Elephant handlers in Nepal use *dana*—bundles of fresh grass, unhusked rice, and molasses—to train and reward their elephants. The Nepalese believe the Hindu elephant god Ganesh resides in every elephant, so dana is not merely a treat, it's an offering.

"We respect the elephants as god, like we respect the god Ganesh," says Satya Narayan, a handler at the Khorsor Hattisar, an elephant stable and training facility in southern Nepal. "We bow to them, like we bow to the god Ganesh. Then we ride them. 'Please forgive us, and protect us as we ride you. We are riding you as an elephant but we know you are a god.'"

The gods can be moody. Handlers need to be able to read and understand their elephant's vocalizations and body language, because a miscalculation with an angry or agitated male elephant weighing 11,000 pounds (5,000 kg) can result in injury and even death for the rider.

Through training methods almost one thousand years old, the elephants learn to respond appropriately to more than twenty-five vocal commands from their handlers, according to Piers Locke, an anthropologist from the University of Canterbury in Christchurch, New Zealand, who works with the handlers at Khorsor Hattisar. In addition to the vocal commands, handlers steer the elephants by pressing their feet behind the elephant's ears.

Narayan describes how communication between elephant and handler evolves. "Slowly the elephants start to understand our language. In their minds they start to understand why we are doing what we do and they start remembering our commands. They start to lie down, to sit, and to walk."

This two-way communication is being put to work, not just in tourism, which gives impoverished Nepalese a livelihood, but in important conservation work. Rangers riding elephants can patrol for poachers and conduct biodiversity surveys in remote places that would otherwise be inaccessible.

Chandra Man Tamang (LEFT), head of the Elephant Breeding Centre, works with a Nepalese elephant handler to train a young male elephant during a workshop. The workshop's aim is to teach elephant trainers to train elephants using gentler techniques and a rewards system instead of punishment.

Telkanranta believes research into elephant communication and family life can shape new methods of training and handling working elephants. Besides helping the elephants learn faster, the new methods prevent a buildup of aggression in them. This makes the elephants safer to work with. "The concepts are easy to understand when seen in practice," Telkanranta says, "and I greatly admire the open-mindedness of the Nepali mahouts who have embraced this new training approach."

REDUCING CONFLICT OVER CROPS

Elsewhere, working elephants are being enlisted to help reduce human-elephant conflict. In Sumatra, logging along the edge of Tesso Nilo National Park is driving elephants to nearby cropland in search of food. The World Wildlife Fund is using captive elephants on poaching patrols and on an Elephant Flying Squad, a rapid response team, to prevent crop raiding. The Flying Squad of nine men and four elephants patrol to spot and intercept crop-raiding elephants and then use noisemakers to herd them back to parkland.

Conservationists and park rangers are working with elephant researchers to put the science of elephant communication to work to reduce elephants' raids on farmers' crops. Early efforts included playing back recordings of elephant alarm calls, but researchers worry that highly intelligent elephants might become accustomed to the recording and ignore it. They also worry that broadcasting recordings could interfere with the elephants' natural communications.

One alternative is using vibration as a way to deter elephants from raiding crops. In Etosha National Park in Namibia, Caitlin O'Connell-Rodwell is working with park rangers to see if the vibration call of a female elephant can lure bulls away from fields of ripe corn. Early tests show the female's estrus rumble played through the ground is enough to make a male elephant turn around and head in the opposite direction.

Elephant scouts learn to identify and monitor individual elephants, especially troublemakers that break fences to raid crops. Studying the elephants' way of life firsthand helps local people manage elephants without resorting to lethal measures.

Kenyan farmers construct beehive fences in areas where elephants are known to raid crops. This strategy was devised by Lucy King of Oxford University in Britain and was implemented with help from Save the Elephants to improve relations between humans and elephants.

These high-tech solutions can only work alongside low-tech efforts by the local farmers and rural villagers. Solutions have to be inexpensive and easy to implement. Conservation groups in northern Kenya are testing all kinds of ideas. One involves stringing beehives on fences to create a barrier elephants hesitate to cross. Others include burning mud bricks spiked with chilies to create clouds of elephant-repellent smoke or changing the spacing and pattern of crops to make them less attractive to elephants. Local community scouts with the Laikipia Elephant Project are even using theater and comic books to bring their message into rural communities.

Researchers have scanned more than one thousand elephant calls looking for a signature crop-raiding call that might alert farmers to an upcoming raid. So far they haven't found one. But the recordings did reveal that elephants were gathering at the same staging area right before a raid, where they would mingle and call to one another. By learning more about this "chatter" as the elephants gather in these staging areas, researchers might be able to give farmers advance warning and time to set up noisemakers to drive elephants from their fields.

LEARNING TO LIVE TOGETHER

PROFILE: Charles Kinyua, elephant scout, Laikipia, northern Kenya

Charles Kinyua *(right)* is an elephant scout with the Laikipia Elephant Project (LEP) in northern Kenya. He and the other scouts use methods pioneered by researchers Iain Douglas-Hamilton and Cynthia Moss to identify and monitor bull elephants. It's these elephants that most often damage fences and destroy crops.

Each scout patrols the 39 square miles (100 sq. km) of territory and calls headquarters when he finds elephant damage to a fence or evidence of crop raiding. LEP staff dash to the site on motorbikes and follow the elephant's footprints to determine which male is responsible. They've learned that thirteen bulls are responsible for 100 percent of the fence breaks. They use their tusks, which don't conduct electricity, to break through the electrified wire. Traditionally these crop-raiding bulls would be killed, but Kinyua and the other scouts are promoting non-deadly ways to stop the fence breakers. These include fitting them with collars that send a text message when the elephant approaches the fence and trimming the bulls' tusks so they can't damage the fences.

The twenty-one scouts receive a salary, but most work part-time, balancing scout duties and meetings with their usual day jobs. The scouts on poaching patrol work full-time. There are plans to hire another nine full-time scouts to help cope with a rise in poaching in the area.

"The relationship between human beings and elephants is good except when the elephants destroy their crops, harm or kill human beings or their animals," says Kinyua. "If human beings and elephants can learn how to live together, their relationship would be very good."

Part of the scouts' job is to teach people to live alongside elephants. Elephant scouts like Kinyua serve as ambassadors between the wildlife management authorities and local people. In places like Laikipia, local politicians often campaign against wildlife conservation to open the land to more farming and other commercial ventures. Conservation workers have been harassed and even attacked by their followers. For conservation to work here, elephant scouts have to protect the livelihoods and lives of local people. They also have to educate them about the value of conservation, not just for the good of elephants but for the good of the land on which they live.

To do this, they set up village fence committees to involve local people directly in elephant management. The scouts also show villagers ways to make a livelihood from elephant crafts such as handmade elephant dung paper. Elephant scouts even bring their conservation message into villages in the form of theater—the scout in the elephant costume has to walk backward into an electric fence!

Scouts like Kinyua are enlisting local farm families to save Kenya's last free-ranging elephants and the ecosystem they inhabit for the benefit of both elephants and people.

Women in rural Kenya make paper from elephant dung (it's mostly grass, so it's not smelly). This provides local Kenyans with a livelihood while helping to protect the elephants.

Elephants use communication to coordinate their movements between feeding grounds. As researchers decode more of the elephants' complex language, future ways of saving both elephants and farmers' livelihoods may emerge.

KEEPING TABS ON ELEPHANTS AND POACHERS

Research by Katy Payne and other scientists with the Elephant Listening Project has shown that elephants vary their calls depending on the size of the herd and its makeup and whether the females in the herd are ready to mate. Payne and her colleagues wondered whether these calling patterns could be used to create a remote monitoring system to check on the well-being of populations of forest elephants in Ghana. Early results are promising, and in the future, networks of recording devices may allow conservationists and ecologists to gather crucial data about the size and makeup of forest elephant populations. The listening posts have added benefits. They can alert conservationists and game wardens to the presence of other vocal species and tip them off to human activity, such as poaching.

In Zambia an organization called Community Markets for Conservation (COMACO) is paying poachers not to poach and is teaching them new trades such as carpentry and beekeeping. It's a cost-effective program. For the cost of catching and prosecuting a single poacher, COMACO can educate and retrain 7 others. So far 350 former poachers have been given new livelihoods, and Zambia's elephants have been given new hope.

BETTER ELEPHANT BIRTHS IN CAPTIVITY

About two o'clock on Valentine's Day morning in 2010, a wild, happy celebration broke out among the African elephant herd at the Wild Animal Park of the San Diego Zoo. It was the sound of the herd welcoming the birth of a new calf. The mother, Ndlula, gave birth out in the open, just as she would in the wild, surrounded and watched over by the rest of the herd.

Ndlula and the other elephants had been airlifted to San Diego in 2003, rescued from a scheduled cull in Swaziland, Africa. The zoo staff was delighted with the birth. The new calf was a sign that the herd was adjusting to its new habitat. Mother and baby were being guarded, as they would be in a wild herd. All these actions indicated that the herd was functioning like a healthy elephant society.

Three baby elephants were born at the San Diego Zoo in 2010. This baby African elephant was born to first time mother Swazi on April 13, 2010.

Making zoo settings and routines more like elephant life in the wild is crucial to maintaining healthy, breeding zoo populations. Zoos are using the latest findings about elephant communication and social structure to provide habitats in which elephants are more likely to breed, conceive, give birth, and raise healthy calves.

CAUTIOUS HOPE

All of these new approaches to conservation offer reason for cautious hope. But elephants are sending us a message, and it's clearly an SOS. Without an end to poaching and habitat destruction, it's possible elephants could be extinct in the wild in our lifetimes. It's not clear why the mammoth became extinct, but if elephants vanish from Earth, there will be no doubt that it was humans who pushed them over the brink.

"SOMETHING DIFFERENT EACH DAY"

PROFILE: Cassie Rogge, elephant keeper, Arizona

Cassie Rogge works with two elephants at the Reid Park Zoo in Tucson, Arizona. Flexible barriers allow her to touch the elephants, but she and the other keepers are not intruding on the animals' space and remain safely separated by cables and bars.

"It took me a year to be accepted as an elephant trainer," Rogge says. "Elephants are herd animals. Some elephants take a long time to accept and trust a new human herd member. Some people never make it into their 'herd.'"

Cassie Rogge gives elephants Shaba (LEFT) and Connie (RIGHT) a cool shower from a hose.

The zookeeper-elephant bond is established through trust and positive reinforcement. Rogge has a different and complex relationship with each elephant in her care.

"Connie, our forty-one-year-old Asian, and I are very vocal with each other. She responds affectionately with grumbles, chirps, and drumming her trunk. There is a lot said in her eyes, too. She is clear in expressing intentions and emotions with us—whether she wants attention, to go inside, is frustrated with a foot-care routine, or just needs some time alone." Although Connie is a very affectionate elephant, she will only accept and cooperate with four of the zoo's keepers.

Rogge also works with Shaba, a thirty-year-old African savanna elephant. "Shaba is smart and eager to take part in training sessions," Rogge says. "She is highly motivated by food rewards!" While Shaba is less vocal and tactile than Connie, she is very observant and keyed into her trainers. At least, until she receives a special treat. "Then she zones out, slowly sucks on it, closes her eyes, and goes catatonic until the treat is gone. During training sessions, Shaba has figured out how to manipulate us into giving her more treats."

Rogge has experienced elephant infrasound firsthand. "On good days, I am greeted with a grumble. Their grumbles range from inaudible to the sound of a truck engine. Sometimes when they are very content, I can feel and hear this deep vibration. . . .

"It's my job to keep the elephants entertained through enrichment and environmental stimulation. We use scents, sounds, puzzles, training, toys, and textures, and [we] present their food in new and different ways to keep them interested. Connie has an enormous industrial-strength ball that she adopted and escorts around the exhibits. It is our goal to make something different happen each day.

"Yet, with all this, one of the elephants' favorite things is just having us stand near them. The elephant-human relationship is fundamental for both their and our health and well-being."

AUTHOR'S NOTE

A s I was finishing this book, I realized that I had spent much of the previous twelve months talking to elephant experts, tracking down facts, and conducting research in libraries and on the Internet. I'd listened to recordings of elephant vocalizations and watched elephants on DVDs and looked at thousands of elephant images. But I hadn't seen a single real live elephant. The last time I'd seen an elephant had been during a visit to the National Zoo in 2005.

I called the Buttonwood Park Zoo in New Bedford, Massachusetts, and one sunny March morning, I drove down to keep a date with their two Asian elephants, Emily and Ruth. I spent the morning observing the interactions between the elephant barn staff and the elephants. I noticed how Ruthie and Emily vocalized and used body language in just the ways I'd been learning about. I didn't get to feel an infrasonic rumble firsthand, but it was pretty thrilling all the same.

But mostly I had come to the zoo hoping to find a way to end this book. What could I say, when the prospects for elephants everywhere seem so dire? As Ruthie explored my fleece and backpack with her trunk, I was at some level hoping the elephants would tell me. But they just munched on banana leaves and regarded me with their long-lashed, amber eyes.

Afterward, I leaned on the rail of the elephant exhibit and spoke to zoo director Bill Langbauer. He knows his elephants. When he's not at the Buttonwood Zoo, he's often conducting elephant research in Kruger National Park in South Africa. I asked him what he thought about the trend to close elephant exhibits and move elephants to sanctuaries. Was there still a place for elephants in zoos?

Langbauer told me that there is no wild left. In their natural range, elephants are under pressure from poaching, habitat loss, and diseases such as elephant tuberculosis. But elephants aren't just refugees in zoos. They play an active role in shaping the next generation of conservationists.

"One of the biggest predictors for growing up to have a conservation ethic is having an 'Oh, Wow,' wildlife experience as a kid," Langbauer told me. "And elephants are about as 'Oh, wow,' as you get." Elephants are big, and they make a big and lasting impression, which we carry throughout our lives, if we're lucky.

As Langbauer and I spoke, Emily calmly stretched her trunk across the moat to pluck at the verge of grass. Young parents came up holding toddlers by the hand and pushing even younger kids in strollers. Here was the beginning of the next generation getting their "Oh, wow" wildlife experience.

Here is the author having her own "Oh, wow" wildlife experience as a child on the back of an Asian elephant in Bangkok, Thailand, in 1972.

But elephants may not have time to wait for these kids to grow up and take action. They need your help today. Find out what you can do to help elephants.

HOW TO HELP THE WORLD'S ELEPHANTS

It goes without saying not to buy ivory. But it's just as important to know where products such as coffee and wood for flooring and furniture come from. The elephants' shrinking habitat is further destroyed by new coffee and timber plantations. Make sure your family buys Forest Stewardship Council (FSC) certified timber and certified fair trade coffee. If you aren't sure whether a product has been grown in a way to sustain forests, ask. You can check the FSC database of participating retailers here:

Forest Stewardship Council-U.S. (FSC-US)
212 Third Avenue North, Suite 280
Minneapolis, MN 55401
http://www.fscus.org/productsearch/retailers/

To help elephants more directly, check out the following organizations:

David Sheldrick Wildlife Trust
http://www.sheldrickwildlifetrust.org/asp/fostering.asp
Foster a savanna elephant online through the David Sheldrick Wildlife Trust in Nairobi, Kenya.

Elephant Care International
166 Limo View Lane
Hohenwald, TN 38462
http://www.elephantcare.org
Support the work of Elephant Care International, a nongovernmental organization (NGO) working in rural villages in Asia and Africa to reduce human-elephant conflict. Your school or youth group can adopt a village to help continue this important work.

Elephant Trails Campaign of the National Zoo

http://nationalzoo.si.edu/Support/AnnualAppeal/ElephantTrek/default.cfm

Support the campaign to improve the welfare of both wild and captive Asian elephants. You can also adopt an Asian elephant.

Roots & Shoots-USA National Office

The Jane Goodall Institute

4245 N. Fairfax Dr., Suite 600

Arlington, VA 22203

http://www.rootsandshoots.org

Join or start a local Roots and Shoots group to work for animals locally and globally. Roots and Shoots was founded in 1992 by sixteen teenagers in Tanzania and promoted by Jane Goodall. It has grown to chapters in nearly one hundred countries. If you're in high school, you can join the Roots and Shoots Youth Leadership Council. The Roots and Shoots website lists lots of ways teens can get involved in conservation and pursue careers to help elephants and other wildlife.

Save the Elephants

P.O. Box 54667

Nairobi 00200

Kenya

http://www.savetheelephants.org

Donate to Save the Elephants, based in Nairobi, Kenya.

Below are the most common elephant call types and some of the ways they are used. Those marked with an L originate in the elephant's larynx. Calls marked with a T originate in the trunk.

chirp (L): used only by Asian elephants and by one captive African savanna elephant that learned to imitate its zoo mates

grunt (L): a short beep or a honk used most often by elephants in the first weeks of life

husky cry (L): Used by younger calves when frightened or separated from the rest of the herd. This cry brings the adult members of the herd running to see what's wrong.

rev (L): A short, high buzz, usually lasting less than a second, and often followed immediately by a rumble. Very rare in wild elephants, this call may mostly be used by captive elephants.

roar (L): A shriek or a scream in young calves, more of a loud bellow in older elephants. This call is also used by a female trying to escape the attentions of an unwanted suitor.

rumbles (L): Elephants use rumbles in many different ways: calves use this call to beg to nurse. Their mothers may rumble to reassure them. The matriarch uses her own special "Let's go" rumble to tell the herd to move out.

scream (L): A shriek in adults that indicates extreme fear and alarm. It was recorded at Amboseli when a lion attacked a calf.

snort (T): A short blast of air through the trunk. This call can signal surprise, alert other members of the herd, or express excitement.

trumpets (T): Another versatile call, used to protest when shoved by another elephant or to frighten away a lion or a hyena. Some can sound like a tuba or a man blowing his nose!

SOURCE NOTES

30 Atiya Y. Hakeem, personal communication with author, April 5, 2010.

42 Angela Stöger-Horwath, personal communication with author, March 7, 2010.

47 Katherine B. Payne, *Silent Thunder: In the Presence of Elephants* (New York: Simon and Schuster, 1998), 28.

47 Ibid., 44.

49 Michael Garstang, personal communication with author, March 22, 2010.

60 Payne, 19–21.

67 David Greenwood, personal communication with author, March 30, 2010.

87 Chandra Man Tamang, personal communication with author, May 6, 2010.

88 Satya Narayan, quoted in Mark Dugas and Piers Locke, *Servants of Ganesh* documentary film transcript (Boston: One World Films, 2009).

89 Helen Telkanranta, personal communication with author, May 6, 2010.

92 Charles Kinyua, personal communication with author, April 6, 2010.

96–97 Cassie Rogge, personal communication with author, March 18, 2010.

99 William Langbauer, personal communication with author, March 9, 2010.

Bates, Lucy A., Katito N. Sayialel, Norah W. Njiraini, Cynthia J. Moss, Joyce H. Poole, and Richard W. Byrne. "Elephants Classify Human Ethnic Groups by Odor and Garment." *Current Biology* 17 (2007): 1,938–1,942.

Bhalla, Nita. "India's 'Toxic' Hindu Idols Choke Rivers: Activists." Reuters, September 25, 2007. http://uk.reuters.com/article/idUKDEL58355200 70925?pageNumber=1 (March 29, 2010).

Casey, Michael, William Foreman, and Jason Straziuso. "African Elephants Imperiled by Ivory Trade in Asia." *LA Times*. 2010. http://latimesblogs .latimes.com/unleashed/2010/05/african-elephants-asian-ivory.html (June 1, 2010).

Chatterjee, Sujoy, and Prashant Mehta. "Indian Festivals: A Time for Celebration or Impending Environmental Disaster: A Comprehensive Analysis." Paper presented at the 97th Indian Science Congress, Thiruvananthapuram, Kerala, India, January 2010.

Chen, Ingfei. "Brain Cells for Socializing." *Smithsonian Magazine*. June 2009. http://www.smithsonianmag.com/science-nature/The-Social-Brain.html (March 20, 2010).

Chevalier-Skolnikoff, Suzanne, and Jo Liska. "Tool Use by Wild and Captive Elephants." *Animal Behaviour* 46 (1993): 209–219.

Cohn, Jeffrey P. "The Social Lives of Savanna Elephants." *Zoogoer*, July–August 2007. http://nationalzoo.si.edu/Publications/ZooGoer/2007/4/ elephant_kinship.cfm (March 29, 2010).

Cornell Lab of Ornithology. "Tools of the (Infrasonic) Trade." Elephant Listening Project. 2009.http://www.birds.cornell.edu/brp/elephant/sections/ field/tools.html (March 29, 2010).

———. "What Is a Sound Spectrogram?" Bioacoustics Research Program. 2010. http://www.birds.cornell.edu/brp/the-science-of-sound-1/ what-is-a-spectrogram (December 31, 2009).

Couzin, Iain. "Behavioral Ecology: Social Organization in Fusion-Fission Societies." *Current Biology* 16 (2006): R169–R171.

Encyclopedia of Life. *Loxodonta cyclotis* (Matschie, 1900). *Encyclopedia of Life*, 2010. http://www.eol.org/pages/289547 (October 7, 2010).

Fox, Douglas. "Case Study: The Elephant Listening Project." *Conservation* Summer 2004, 30–37.

Garstang, Michael. "Long-Distance, Low-Frequency Elephant Communication." *Journal of Comparative Physiology* A 190 (2004): 791–805.

Granli, Petter, and Joyce Poole. "About ElephantVoices." ElephantVoices. 2010. http://www.elephantvoices.org (March 18, 2010).

Groning, Karl, and Martin Saller. *Elephants: A Cultural and Natural History*. New York: Konemann, 1999.

Hambling, David. "Robotic Tentacles Get to Grips with Tricky Objects." *New Scientist*, May 8, 2006. http://www.newscientist.com/article/dn9124 -robotic-tentacles-get-to-grips-with-tricky-objects.html (July 8, 2009).

Hart, B. L., L. A. Hart, and N. Pinter-Wollman. "Large Brains and Cognition: Where Do Elephants Fit In?" *Neuroscience & Biobehavioral Reviews* 32 (2008): 86–98.

Hill, Peggy S. M. "Vibration and Animal Communication: A Review." *American Zoologist* 41 (2001): 1,135–1,142.

Kahl, M. Philip, and Billie D. Armstong. "Visual Displays of Wild African Elephants during Musth." *Mammalia* 66, no. 2 (2002): 361–363.

Morgan, James. "Vibrations Could Save Elephants. BBC News Online. February 14, 2009. http://news.bbc.co.uk/2/hi/science/ nature/7890919.stm (May 20, 2010).

Nowak, Ronald, ed. *Walker's Mammals of the World*, 6th ed. Baltimore: Johns Hopkins University Press, 1999.

O'Connell-Rodwell, Caitlin. *The Elephant's Secret Sense: The Hidden Life of the Wild Herds of Africa*. New York: Free Press, 2007.

———. "Keeping an 'Ear' to the Ground: Seismic Communication in Elephants." *Physiology* 22 (2007): 287–294.

Payne, Katherine B. *Silent Thunder: In the Presence of Elephants*. New York: Simon and Schuster, 1998.

———. "Sources of Social Complexity in the Three Elephant Species." In *Animal Social Complexity: Intelligence, Culture, and Individualized Societies,* edited by Frans B. M. DeWaal and Peter L. Tyack. Cambridge, MA: Harvard University Press, 2003.

Payne, Katherine B., William R. Langbauer Jr., and Elizabeth Thomas. "Infrasonic Calls of the Asian Elephant (*Elephas maximus*)." *Behavioral Ecology and Sociobiology* 18 (1986): 297–301.

Rasmussen, L. E. L., and V. Krishnamurthy. "How Chemical Signals Integrate Asian Elephant Society: The Known and the Unknown." *Zoo Biology* 19 (2000): 405–423.

Rasmussen, L. E. L., J. Lazar, and D. R. Greenwood. "Olfactory Adventures of Elephantine Pheromones." *Biochemical Society Transactions* 31 (2003): 137–141.

Rasmussen L. E. L., and B. L. Munger. "The Sensorineural Specializations of the Trunk Tip (Finger) of the Asian Elephant, *Elephas maximus*." *Anatomical Record* 246 (1996): 127–134.

Rohland, N., A. S. Malaspinas, J. L. Pollack, M. Slatkin, P. Matheus, and H. Hofreiter. "Proboscidean Mitogenomics: Chronology and Mode of Elephant Evolution Using Mastodon as Outgroup." *Library of Science: Biology* 5, no. 8 (August 2007): 207.

Schatz, Joseph J. "A Cheaper Plan to Stop Poachers: Give Them Real Jobs." *Christian Science Monitor*, October 23, 2007. http://www.csmonitor.com/2007/1023/p01s07-woaf.html (May 20, 2010).

Schulte, B. A., Kathryn Bagley, Maureen Correll, Amy Gray, Sarah M. Heineman, Helen Loizi, Michelle Malament, et al, "Assessing Chemical Communication in Elephants." In *Chemical Signals in Vertebrates*. Vol. 10, edited by Robert T. Mason, Michael P. LeMaster, and Dietland Müller-Schwarze. New York: Springer-Verlag, 2005.

Schulz, Katja, ed. *Elephas maximus Linnaeus*, 1758. *Encyclopedia of Life*. 2010. http://www.eol.org/pages/997407 (September 15, 2010).

———. *Loxodonta Africana* (Blumenbach, 1797). *Encyclopedia of Life*, 2010. http://www.eol.org/pages/289808 (September 15, 2010).

———. *Loxodonta cyclotis* (Matschie, 1900). *Encyclopedia of Life*. 2010. http://www.eol.org/pages/289547 (September 15, 2010).

Shoshani, Jeheskel, and Pascal Tassy, eds. *The Proboscidea: Evolution and Ecology of Elephants and Their Relatives*. New York: Oxford University Press, 1996.

Sikes, Sylvia K. *The Natural History of the African Elephant*. London: Weidenfeld & Nicholson, 1971.

Slotow, Rob, Gus van Dyk, Joyce Poole, Bruce Page, and Andrew Klocke. "Older Bull Elephants Control Young Males." *Nature* 408 (2000): 425–426.

Sukumar, Raman. *The Living Elephants: Evolutionary Ecology, Behavior, and Conservation*. Oxford: Oxford University Press, 2003.

Thompson, Mya E., Seven J. Schwager, Katherine B. Payne, and Andrea K. Turkalo. "Acoustic Estimation of Wildlife Abundance: Methodology for Vocal Mammals in Forested Habitats." *African Journal of Ecology*, September 2009, 654–661.

Walker, John Frederick. *Ivory's Ghosts: The White Gold of History and the Fate of Elephants*. New York: Grove Press, 2009.

Wasser, Samuel K., Bill Clark, and Cathy Laurie. "The Ivory Trail." *Scientific American*, July 2009, 68–74.

World Wildlife Fund. "Sumatra and Borneo: Elephant Flying Squad." WWF. 2010. http://www.worldwildlife.org/what/wherewework/borneo/elephantflyingsquad.html (March 30, 2010).

FURTHER READING AND WEBSITES

Books

Agenbroad, Larry, and Lisa Nelson: *Mammoths: Ice Age Giants*. Minneapolis: Twenty-First Century Books, 2002.

Allman, Toney. *Animal Life in Groups*. New York: Chelsea House, 2009.

Bloom, Steve. *Elephant*. San Francisco: Chronicle Books, 2006.

Cox, Barry. Updated by Douglas Palmer. *The Simon & Schuster Encyclopedia of Dinosaurs and Prehistoric Creatures: A Visual Who's Who of Prehistoric Life*. New York: Simon and Schuster, 1999.

Darling, Kathy, and Tara Darling. *The Elephant Hospital*. Minneapolis: Millbrook Press, 2000.

Facklam, Margery. *Bees Dance and Whales Sing: The Mysteries of Animal Communication*. San Francisco: Sierra Club Books, 2001.

Joubert, Dereck, and Beverly Joubert. *Face to Face with Elephants*. Washington, DC: National Geographic, 2008.

Kalman, Bobbie. *Endangered Elephants*. New York: Crabtree Publishing, 2005.

Lewin, Ted, and Betsy Lewin. *Balarama: A Royal Elephant*. New York: Lee & Low, 2009.

Morgan, Jody. *Elephant Rescue: Changing the Future for Endangered Wildlife*. Buffalo: Firefly Books, 2004.

Owen, Marna. *Animal Rights: Noble Cause or Needless Effort?* Minneapolis: Twenty-First Century Books, 2010.

Pringle, Laurence. *Elephant Woman: Cynthia Moss Explores the World of Elephants*. New York: Atheneum Books for Young Readers, 1997.

Sayre, April Pulley. *Secrets of Sound: Studying the Calls and Sounds of Whales, Elephants, and Birds*. Boston: Sandpiper Books, 2006.

Shoshani, Jeheskel, ed. *Elephants: Majestic Creatures of the Wild*. New York: Facts on File, 2000.

Woods, Michael, and Mary B. Woods. *Ancient Transportation Technology*. Minneapolis: Twenty-First Century Books, 2011.

Websites

Amboseli Trust for Elephants
   http://www.elephanttrust.org/
   The Amboseli Elephant Research Project focuses on the lives and futures of fifteen hundred elephants in the Amboseli ecosystem near Mount Kilimanjaro in Kenya.

Elephant Listening Project at Cornell
   http://www. birds.cornell.edu/brp/
   elephant/
   Find information about the research of Katy Payne and the development of elephant listening devices.

Elephant Voices
   http://www.elephantvoices.org
   This site has links to play elephant trumpets and rumbles and other calls.

Physics Classroom
   http://www.physicsclassroom.com/
   class/sound/
   A good online resource for the physics of sound can be found here.

Expand learning beyond the printed book. Download free, complementary educational resources for this book from our website, www.lerneresource.com.

INDEX

AUTHOR'S ACKNOWLEDGMENTS

The following people were incredibly generous with their insight, expertise, and time, providing images and quotes, helping me to track down other people, steering me to sources I'd overlooked, and checking facts. The views expressed in this book are my own.

Ronnie Broadfoot, Dana Fisher, and Mary Sears, Ernst Mayr Library, Harvard University; David R. Greenwood, University of Auckland; Michael Garstang, University of Virginia; Max Graham and Joseph Kariuki, Laipikia Elephant Project, Kenya; Atiya Y. Hakeem, Allman Lab, California Institute of Technology; Darlene Ketten, Woods Hole Oceanographic Institution; William Langbauer, director, Buttonwood Park Zoo, New Bedford, Massachusetts; Piers Locke, University of Canterbury, Christchurch, New Zealand; Caitlin O'Connell-Rodwell, Stanford University; Steve Osofsky, Wildlife Conservation Society; Cassie Rogge, zookeeper, Reid Park Zoo, Tucson, Arizona; Liz D. Rowland, the Elephant Listening Project; Bruce Schulte, Western Kentucky University; Meike Artelt and Angela Stöger-Horwath, Mammal Communication Lab, University of Vienna and Zoo Vienna; Matt Walpole, United Nations Monitoring Programme—World Conservation Monitoring Centre. The quotation from elephant handler Satya Narayan is used with kind permission of One World Films, whose producer, Mark Dugas, generously shared with me the rough cut of his documentary about mahouts in Nepal, *Servants of Ganesh*. Daniel Hartline of the Békésy Laboratory of Neurobiology at the University of Hawaii and Dr. Robert Cole were helpful in confirming the anecdote about Georg von Békésy and the elephant's ears. The Buttonwood Zoo in New Bedford, Massachusetts, generously provided access to their two Asian elephants, Emily and Ruth. After an unforgettable afternoon with them, I left the elephant barn covered in elephant sneeze but energized and inspired for my final push to complete the book.

Marcia Marshall, my editor, was just as marvelous as I remembered from our work together on my first three and a half books. I felt so very lucky to be able to work with her again at Lerner and benefit from her warmth and wisdom one more time. Martha Kranes shepherded the book through production, with assistance from photo researcher Erica Johnson and illustrator Laura Westlund. Designer Amelia LeBarron's beautiful design brought elephants and their fascinating science vividly to life on the page.

Finally, thanks to my husband and son for their unwavering support and forbearance as I logged endless hours with my laptop, peppered every conversation with elephant facts, and answered most queries with a distracted "Uh huh–What?" You are my herd.

ABOUT THE AUTHOR

Ann Downer's interest in elephants started in childhood, when she witnessed an elephant roundup in Thailand on her twelfth birthday. A former science editor at Harvard University Press, she worked with world-renowned biologists and nature photographers to develop books on topics such as earwig mothers, glow-in-the-dark jellyfish, smart parrots, and the use of insect evidence to solve crimes. Downer is the author of two books with the New England Aquarium, *Don't Blink Now: Capturing the Hidden World of Sea Creatures*, and the award-winning *Spring Pool: A Guide to the Ecology of Temporary Ponds*. Her latest venture is assisting with the educational outreach for the Encyclopedia of Life, the worldwide effort to put information about almost 2 million known species on Earth online (www.eol.org). She lives in Somerville, Massachusetts.

PHOTO ACKNOWLEDGMENTS